PURE FABRICATION

PURE FABRICATION

Fabric ideas for the home

Maggie Colvin

CHILTON BOOK COMPANY
Radnor Pennsylvania

Copyright © The Rainbird Publishing Group Ltd 1985

All Rights Reserved

Published in Radnor, Pennsylvania 19089 by
Chilton Book Company

This book was designed and produced by
The Rainbird Publishing Group Ltd
27 Wrights Lane
London W8 5TZ

Contributors: Deborah Evans, Hilary More, Gillian Rothwell
Illustrators: Jane Cradock Watson, Alicia Durdos, Carole Johnson
Editor: Charyn Jones
Designer: Sally Smallwood

First published 1985
Reprinted 1986
Reprinted 1988
Manufactured in Italy
Library of Congress Card Catalog Number 84 71909

ISBN 0 8019 7603 0

Text set by Bookworm Typesetting, Manchester, England
Illustrations originated by Totographics Limited, Hong Kong
Printed and bound by Arnoldo Mondadori Editore, Verona, Italy

CONTENTS

INTRODUCTION

For many of us the fabric counters in large department stores are magnetic, irresistible hunting grounds to which we are drawn like bees to a honey pot. It is not just the sheer delight of savouring the deep, sizzling colours or the pretty patterns, it is also the wealth of textures – the crunchiness of glazed cotton, the soft, weightlessness of Thai silk or the nobbly richness of home-spun wool. After all, nobody buys a fabric without first touching it.

However, the overriding appeal of any fabric lies in its potential. A length of Liberty print can offer limitless opportunity. A fresh red and white polka-dot cotton would make pretty frilled cushion covers on a window seat in an otherwise all-white kitchen. Or would green gingham make more impact? A deep rust Victorian velvet could be just what is needed to cover a piano stool. A length of deep rich turquoise raw silk would surely make beautiful quilted cushions piped in green. This book is designed to inspire you to exploit the full potential of the fabrics you fall in love with, and possibly already have collected. They are just waiting to be sewn into something special.

When it comes to decorating, fabric is undoubtedly an easier option for those not interested in or adept at carpentry. Given yards of fabric translated into curtains and drapes, it is possible to achieve dramatic changes, equal to those wrought by any carpenter. With a pretty pair of curtains you can 'build' a cupboard, or cordon off part of the room. With a generous roll of fabric you can turn a dreary little room into draped luxury with a tented ceiling. Depending on your window-dressing imagination, you can alter the shape and style of windows, improve the architectural details or hide them altogether.

Fabric is a terrific cover-up; not just for chairs and sofas, but tables, chests and cupboard doors, and even floors and badly plastered walls. It involves a lot less energy and mess to batten the walls and cover the bumps with fabric than to call in the plasterer for a complete overhaul.

Fabric provides an easy and instant method of injecting colour and personality into a room. Analyse a room in need of pepping up and try injecting a splash of some bright new colours, for example in a tablecloth or cushion covers. You will find this course of action far easier, cheaper and possibly more effective.

When it comes to charting a new style for any particular room in the house, fabric is an invaluable pace setter, an inspirational starting point. Whereas some antique lovers will most naturally evolve a colour scheme around an old piece of furniture, or perhaps choose an oriental carpet as their focal point, fabric addicts gravitate to the fabric counters and search for the textile design which embodies the style they are looking for. It could be an eighteenth-century chintz of formalized flowers and bows, or a Bauhaus geometric. Certain fabrics dictate a style so clearly that they make the job of creating a distinct atmosphere easy. For instance, pink and white chintz is bound to convey a comfortable and informal cottage look (see pages 62 and 72); whereas red moiré evokes a rather dusty but rich Edwardian room set.

Mixing colours and patterns is an art in itself. To a talented few it is a skill which seems inborn and, like natural cooks, they apparently pick and mix exactly the right ingredients without being able to say why the mixture works. To others not so blessed, the business of colour and pattern can be quite daunting. After all, a major part of making your own soft furnishings is that, if you can put an indivdual stamp on whatever it is you have sewn, you'll have created something special which money cannot buy.

You may like lots of the ideas in this book, but the colours and patterns simply would not work in your room. Colour is a very personal affair. To help you to find alternative colour schemes and to stimulate your visual instincts, I have outlined some proven colour mixes and pattern recipes which are known to work (see page 17). They are well-documented successes which most interior designers fall back on time and time again.

You don't have to be a skilled sewer. The projects in this book require mainly enthusiasm, patience and the ability to sew forwards in a straight line. Some of the most original ideas are the simplest to make and some of the most effective ideas are also the least expensive. For instance, blanket ribbon can be bound around the edges of worn-out sheets to give extra wear, and by introducing parallel lines of two or three satin ribbons, plain white sheets can be cheerfully coloured in pinks and greens, or yellows and reds, or whatever matches the other colours in the bedroom.

Finally, because it is quite easy to get lost amongst fabric definitions I have included a brief guide to fabrics and fibres and their characteristics at the end of the book (see pages 182-187).

Maggie Colvin

COLOUR AND STYLE

In spite of the probable hazards and frustrations, the effort and expense, most of us welcome the chance to do up a room, if not a whole house. It is part of our nest-building instinct and an accessible means of self expression. The main problem for the beginner is that decorating costs and the effects live with us. Even those who have some idea of the style of room they would like, are not always sure how to achieve it. Others prefer someone else to decide for them, and there is a rare handful of confident, clear thinkers who know exactly what they want, and can translate their vision into reality down to the last carefully chosen door knob. Undoubtedly the results of their vision leave the majority of us breathless, wishing somehow that we could achieve that kind of stylish perfection and finish.

To be successful you have to decide what you want and stick to it and this requires careful planning. Even if you are not decorating the whole room from scratch it is vital to have worked out a detailed picture before you begin your shopping – where the seating will be, what colours will go where, and even what kind of lights would be best. Without this clear overview the shop floor, with its enticing displays and endless choice, can prove your downfall.

Finding the style

Developing a style of your own is often a question of confidence, though experience certainly helps. The wisest, most conscientious observers learn by analysing other people's successes and failures. They leaf through magazines and books, visit historic houses, lift colour-scheme ideas from pictures in art galleries and museums. Their eye for detail is insatiable. Even in restaurants and shops they scrutinize the light fittings, the type of panelling or the drape of the curtains. With all these ideas logged in a scrapbook, they will pick out and cheerfully copy the best – and why not? No two ideas ever end up looking exactly the same.

Even if you are not so organized, I think it helps to list the qualities you would like to include in your new decorating scheme, as well as making a note of some mistakes you may have noticed or suffered from yourself. For instance, dark chocolate carpet which looks so smart with chrome and glass furniture shows every speck of fluff. Are you the type to be constantly cleaning? The wallpaper on the ceiling of your bathroom did eventually peel off through condensation. Make a mental note to find a more practical alternative. A burnt-orange painted study, so cosy on wet days, looks dirty in the sunlight and would have been a better choice for a formal dining-room, used mainly at night. An unbroken wall of mirror in a hall works with modern furniture and a cool grey

Bold fabrics used abundantly and with great conviction dictate an updated Bauhaus-style drawing room. This striking and successful mix of colours and patterns is not difficult to achieve if you follow the rules.

carpet, but paired with a carved oak chest and a Moorish rug, it would look better framed and mounted in panels. Reflections of this kind are best remembered and even noted down; it is so easy to forget.

Giving the style a name

In choosing a style for any particular room, it is helpful to remember that certain styles call out for definite colour partners. For instance, Victorian furniture looks at home with dark rich colours; cottagey rooms with oak beams and tiled quarry floors look right in natural colours with a variety of rough rural textures. You can ring the changes and it is fun to

Above A casual but stylish rendering of indoor patio style is carried off here with an almost all-white colour scheme. The delicate tracery of huge leafy plants is echoed in the lacey patterns created by the cane dining chairs and table. The windows are simply dressed with vertical Venetian blinds.

Right Simple, bold and stunning – this room is distinctly international and deliberately severe due to the dedicated and restricted use of black and some white. People become the sole decorative element.

be different, but you do run risks. So even if your style has to incorporate lots of family hand-me-downs and junk you can not afford to replace, it is a good idea to start in an uncompromising frame of mind. Within a well-tried framework, you can safely add the personal touches. Here are some styles that are firm favourites with a rough guide to the ingredients you might include.

Country Cottage Style is nostalgic, comfortable and very pretty and increasingly sought after in a world populated mainly by city dwellers. The chief ingredients are traditional pine, bentwood and wicker furniture. The flag-stone or wooden floors are covered with rugs; there are brass bedsteads and wash stands in the bedroom, and Welsh dressers and refectory tables in the dining-room. The living areas are decorated in a natural colour scheme, with fresh and pretty combinations, like pink, green and white, in the bedrooms. Curtain treatments should be simple and unsophisticated, such as plain lace hangings and café curtains.

Sleek Italian is a more expensive style. It includes chrome and glass tables, and voluptuous upholstered shapes for seating with quilted covers. Floors should be laid with ceramic tiles or a sleek, soberly patterned parquet; rugs and pictures are abstract; lighting is sculptured and flamboyant. Window treatments are plain – vertical louvres, shutters and Venetian blinds – and extremist colour schemes such as black and white, or all white, are sometimes accented by primary colours.

Plush Victorian requires mahogany furniture and buttoned upholstery covered in velvet, leather or damask. Brass beds or fabric four-posters, découpage screens and free-standing wardrobes fill the bedrooms. Carpets, rugs and all soft furnishings should be opulent and patterned; curtains full length, tied-back and pelmeted, or Austrian blinds. Colours should be rich and on the dark side – rose, crimson, plum and olive.

Indoor Patio (or Palm Beach Style) is a mixture of outdoor and indoor furniture and has become increasingly popular with the availability of stylish wicker shapes – some natural, some painted. Large umbrellas and turn-of-the-century wooden or brass fans are also appropriate. Lots of plants, ceramic-tiled floor or coir or coconut matting is essential. For windows, choose lattice- or trellis-patterned shutters or bamboo blinds. Sofa and armchair frames should ideally be rattan, with palm-tree prints or plain white for the seat covers.

Hi-tech is a style full of glossy space-age finishes such as silver, PVC and brightly coloured plastics. Furniture is angular, often incorporating panels of wire mesh. Fabrics tend towards the geometrics, simple checks or evenly dispersed brush strokes in sharp peppermint greens, pinks and yellows. Floors should be unobtrusive – rubber stud or cork. It is a style with an efficient feel to it. Window dressing should be sparse and crisp – corrugated silver or Venetian blinds. Colour schemes are metallic grey with accents in sharp pastels. Silver, red and black is another favourite combination.

Turn of the Century is a cosy, patterned, lived-in look, embellished with old-fashioned lace, silver hair brushes and photograph frames. There are rose-patterned walls, decorative iron bedsteads and patchwork bedspreads thrown over the sofas and chairs as well as the beds. Edwardian furniture and lights are now being reproduced en masse, so you do not have to rely solely on junk shops. Choose faded and romantic colour schemes in old-fashioned colours – old rose rather than fresh tulip pink and so on. Mix patterns, particularly in rugs, or choose a patterned carpet.

Ethnic or Peasant Style is not unlike country cottage, but brighter, and mid-European or Mexican in feeling, with painted furniture in primary colours and an abundant use of stencils to decorate the walls and furniture. Stickback and rocking chairs are covered in knitted rugs and shawls. Floors can be painted or stencilled with braided or rag rugs over them. Painted cupboards and even a baby's wooden cradle would not look out of place in the living-room. Patchwork and check curtains with simple curtain rings sewn directly onto the top hemline are also in keeping.

Thirties Deco is a style to which you must be totally dedicated. To carry it off you have to collect all the right ornaments and furniture of the period. Veneered bedrooms and dining-room suites, round-fronted ash storage units and unframed, arched mirrors are key elements. Typical colour combinations are: grey and peach; grey and mustard; white, black, grey and pink. Fabrics and rugs come in jazzy geometrics, and the wall lights are angular and often made of frosted glass.

Oriental Fantasy demands a tidy life-style. Overtones of chinoiserie have been a part of our culture since the last century and the fashion for silk Chinese paintings, fans, blossom trees, oriental china and rattan furniture persists. Apart from a good collection of Chinese accessories – a large trellis screen, back-lit and covered with perspex (or tracing paper) against one wall, is always a success. Rattan blinds and oriental bird cages are easy to mix in with big floor cushions covered in a Chinese-style print. White and yellow trellis patterns always mix well. Colour schemes should incorporate a good mixture of yellow and black.

An eclectic, some would say eccentric collection of pictures, junk-shop finds and different patterns are unified here by a strong, daring choice of red on the walls. It is a brave and clever choice which diffuses the exact dimensions of the room making it seem cosy but not claustrophobic.

Below The matching tables, chairs and sofas laid out in graceful symmetry give this room an ordered peacefulness and the style of layout is repeated in geometric patterns in the sofa cover, rug and the ceiling over the dining area. Extra sparkle and life is due to the wonderful tomato red in the cushions.

Right A creamy muslin fabric has been used in lavish profusion to produce this piece of Arabian fantasy. It is a good example of how fabric can create a complete room. Everything, except the tables, lamps and accessories, is covered in fabric with visual interest provided by the undulating shapes of the different floor cushions.

Scandinavian Look is based on blond wood floors and furniture and a sparseness of line and colour. White and yellow or yellow and blue are typical of this style. Sheer curtains with simple headings, berber carpets, plain coir matting, or even quarry tiles would work on the floor. Ornamentation consists of candles and bunches of daisies or tulips in clear simple vases in which the pattern of the stems becomes as important as the heads.

Tailored Decorator has walls covered in fabric and edged in braid, and tables and even curtain poles covered in fabric. Decorators tend to excel in this tailored fabric look. They vere

towards smart geometric prints, box pleats and lots of crisp contrasting piping. Round tables with tablecloths to the floor are often piped around the table edges, and skirts are softly box pleated or straight as opposed to frilled. The attention to detail is ordered and considered, and furniture and accessories comply to a formal layout. Whatever the colour scheme – blue and white, or orange and gold – it is always carried consistently through to the last small bowl of matching flowers.

This list is by no means complete. There are mid-Atlantic, traditional English country house, Jacobean, American country formats and others besides. There are also rooms that clearly mix styles and really do not fall into any category. Some rooms happily combine chrome and leather Bauhaus chairs with Victorian commodes and still hang together visually. So many rooms made up of a mixture of styles are richer and more interesting for it. But the business of mixing styles, like mixing patterns, makes the design of a room that much more difficult. Essentially you need a unifying colour scheme.

The right colour scheme
Choosing the right colours for a room is ultimately even more important than collecting the right furniture. Clashing

colours will topple any visual peace and pleasure you might enjoy in a room. Some people put together successful colour schemes easily. They arrange pieces for a patchwork bed-spread as unselfconsciously as picking the right accessories for a suit of clothes. To others, making decisions about colour is fretful and traumatic. Fortunately the more you force your-self to exercise visual instincts, the more confident a colour sense you will develop, and there are also some well-tested, documented successes to fall back on – groups of colours which are guaranteed to work well together.

They are best understood by the colour wheel, which is a wheel of six colours that most people identify as rainbow colours. They are the purest, most solid and intense colours, and they relate to each other via the colour wheel in this order: red, orange, yellow, green, blue, violet. The red, yellow and blue are the primary colours, and the violet, green and orange are known as secondary primaries, so called because they are created by mixing two primaries together; hence red + yellow = orange, yellow + blue = green and blue + red = violet. All other colours, incidentally, are mixed from these six colours with the addition of various quantities of black and white.

The colour wheel may sound a rather abstract and irrelevant concept, but it is a very simple way to work out whether colours will blend or contrast with one another. There are two easy rules to follow: a colour will blend with its neighbour on either side, for instance orange will blend with yellow on one side and red on the other, while colours positioned opposite to one another on the wheel will contrast. So red is in direct contrast to green, and yellow to purple. If you decide to make a new collection of cushion covers, say in blue, then a good choice of piping colour would be green or violet. But if you want a more vibrant combination, then piping in red, orange or yellow would give you a more dazzling, contrasting effect.

Many of the most successful colour schemes, particularly those intended for whole rooms, rely upon the generous use of one background colour, for floor, walls and ceiling, to act as a unifying element. Add a small touch of one or two accent colours and the scheme comes alive. The amount is also vitally important, for the weighting of colours, like ingredients in a recipe, is as important as picking the right combination of colours. For instance, if you colour 50 per cent of a room's surfaces in orange and the remaining 50 per cent in yellow, the tendency for the two colours to fight for attention would detract considerably from the harmony of the scheme, even though orange and yellow lie next to each other on the colour wheel. A more peaceful scheme would comprise of 80 per cent of yellow and 20 per cent of orange. The same theory applies whether you are putting together colours for an appliquéd tablecloth or many fabrics for a braided rug.

Different textile patterns mix happily together in this sitting room, visually held together by the consistent application of a blue and green colour scheme. The generous and tailored use of fabric is typically decorator style, carried out with an easy conviction.

Infallible colour combinations

If you love a certain colour, and colour is very much an affair of the heart, monotone schemes built up entirely in tones of one colour can be as exciting as any other combination, and this is an easy format to put into practice. For extra life and dazzle, add a 15 to 20 per cent proportion of white and you have hit upon an ancient colour recipe that never fails. Tones of blue and white, yellow and white, green and white, red and white and so on have been used to the enjoyment of home makers for centuries.

There are several other colour combinations worth mentioning because of their infallibility, and when you are stuck for inspiration, and trying to sort fabric pieces into suitable colour piles, these are useful standbys:

Rainbow colours (primaries and secondaries). These are loud, punchy colours and need to be used with conviction. They have a happy nature, which is probably why we traditionally use them at Christmas for decorations and for decorating children's rooms. They are associated with the folk art of primitive cultures. Being so hot and dramatic, other colours recede beside them, and if you combine in alternating stripes two rainbow colours like red and blue, you will discover that they tend to 'vibrate'. To quieten the effect, add black or put them against a dark navy background. To dilute and lighten the impact, add a generous amount of white.

All colours are modified by their surrounding colours, which is why it is a good idea to experiment and juxtapose actual colour samples before deciding on a colour scheme. For instance, if you place a bright red appliqué shape against brown, the red appears to soften and becomes less intense. Placed against black, it becomes richer and more sophisticated, against white, crisper and cleaner, and so on.

Pastel colours Pink, peppermint green, lilac, apricot, baby blue and lemon-yellow are soft seductive colours which come from mixing white with the rainbow colours. It is this injection of white which harmonizes pastels and makes them work so well together, like sugar candy or ice cream, which both have a strong white base. The joy of using a pastel

Left *The repetition of a stencil pattern in soft autumn colours on bedcover and window dressings gives this cottage bedroom a unified style. The fabrics are inexpensive woven cottons but the effect is so special and individual that it is priceless.*

Right *Each piece of furniture in this bedroom has a different heritage, making it a difficult style to define. They all, however, have a similar fine quality and feminine line. The dramatic bed canopy dictates the gentle, harmonious colour scheme in tones of creams, yellows and pastels.*

colour scheme is that you really cannot go far wrong. For the maximum effect, incorporate as many pastels as possible, and if you feel the scheme is becoming too sugary and sickly, introduce a surface of plain white; the floor, a bedspread, curtains, etc. Against a white background many colours acquire a special clarity and this is particularly true of the pastels. For instance, a white cotton cushion cover edged in pastel ribbons will enhance the luminosity of the ribbons and the white gaps between the ribbons appear to 'lift' the colours.

There are at least two sure ways to develop a pastel colour scheme. Inject a dash of one of the primary colours — say bright red or orange — for hotter, spicier results. And for a more sophisticated look, add one of the sludge colours — from oatmeal to khaki — but if you choose this route, take care that you do not destroy the inherent gentleness and prettiness of the pastel scheme.

White on white This is a luscious, glamorous, space-expanding recipe, which with easy-to-clean materials, especially for the floors, need not be as impractical to live with as it sounds. People and plants always look good in all-white rooms and even the tiniest ray of sunlight produces a symphony of bright yellow tones which makes the room a joy to sit in. A basement room can even look light and bright.

Textures take on a tremendous importance in a white colour scheme. Quilting and natural brick walls, bubbly yarns and even shiny flat surfaces such as PVC become more prominent. The reverse proves the point. If a cable sweater is knitted in a bright primary colour, the texture of the knitting stitches almost disappears.

Natural neutrals Many of the same rules for white-on-white apply to predominantly beige and off-white schemes. The main difference is that the connection between neutrals and Nature conjures up a home-spun country atmosphere. All-white rooms can, furnished appropriately, look space age. Neutral rooms, in shades of pale browns or sandy pinks, never can. If you look closely at the gradations of grey in a pebble on the beach, or the different shades of pinky beige that span the surface of a sea shell, you will realize just how many colour variations fall within a neutral spectrum and how easily their depth and variety marry. They almost need one another; used singly they can look dull and bland. It is this variety of tones that makes them interesting. To spice up a neutral colour scheme, apricot, burnt orange or bright pink will add warmth without detracting from the relaxing blend. Or for a more sophisticated look, add black or dark navy.

Rich and dark colours It takes a strong nerve to paint walls bright red or dark blue. Most of us are preoccupied with making rooms look light and airy, and dark colours do make a room look smaller. However, they also add a dimension of cosy security and drama, which pays off, particularly at night, when lit with spotlights or uplighters set behind plants. Mirrors, candlelight and shiny objects help inject glitter. Most dark colours are best used on their own, unless you combine them in equal amounts, of equal strength and in quite small quantities, rather as in an oriental carpet.

Pink and green (or apricot and green) When used in equal proportions against a background of white, this is a pretty and refreshing colour combination, particularly popular for country-style bedrooms. It is as soft and appealing as sweet peas, or summer roses in full bloom, and although the precise tones of pink and green are subject to fashion waves – minty green is in one year, apple green the next – it remains a classic colour scheme with good reason.

Blue and green In varying tones, this combination, set against a white or cream background, effects a cool, clear, relaxing atmosphere particularly valuable for hot climates, or south-facing rooms. While pink and green tend always to look pretty and soft, blue and green has a wider scope. Irrespective of style, blue and green in multi-patterned florals look as appropriate in frilly country rooms as in a more tailored, penthouse apartment.

Left This is a textbook example of how one pattern need not overwhelm a room. Its success relies on the blue and white colour scheme, an easy paisley pattern and the additional touch of terracotta in the rug, floor tiles and in the pine and rattan furniture.

Above A colour scheme of pink, green and white is a country classic which inevitably carries charm and fresh prettiness. White cane furniture and white background with the clever choice of textiles and wallpaper give a conservatory character to the room.

Rules of Pattern

Often your choice of textile design or carpet pattern will determine the other colours in the room for you, which is as good as having the scheme dictated by a professional. Even so, you may have the problem of mixing patterns, or indeed you may do so by choice. Skilfully put together, several different patterns add considerably to a room's visual interest, but mixing patterns that 'fight' is the quickest way to turn a room into a visual disaster. Mixing patterns does not come easily, or without risk. Here are three rules you can rely on. Rule number one is to pick fabrics with an equal balance of similar colours, and the colours need to be equal in strength. They could be pastels or primaries or a haphazard mixture. The second rule is to match the rhythm of the patterns you have mixed. For example, it may be geometrics, or mini floral prints, or Indian paisleys. The third and possibly the most effortless rule to follow is to select and then stick staunchly to a definite character theme, such as Chinese, Indian, Art Nouveau, or French Provençal.

It is important to study a fabric from a distance to avoid putting it into the wrong category. For instance, a small recurring floral print, which looks quite florid close up, may well lose definition from a distance and acquire a textural geometric softness which will happily mix with most large-scale patterns, provided they share a colour theme.

Finally, it is easy to forget that patterns are also produced by furniture, plants, books and other objects in the room and, if possible, they should enhance and amplify the character of textile patterns. Curvy armchairs, for instance, obviously look happier covered in swirly, curvy florals. Visual similarities of this kind always help to make a room hang together.

Lighting Consideration

Your choice of lighting will also affect the colours in a room, and it is important not to leave decisions about lighting too late. After all any re-wiring needs to be done before final decorating. So often, especially in new houses, a central light and a haphazard smattering of power points are installed without question, although most people find the central light source as bland and as tiring on the eyes as a foggy grey day, and the electrical points are seldom where they are most needed.

Lighting should provide background light, local light for a particular purpose, and decorative light for atmosphere or decorative effect. All colours alter slightly in artificial light; blues and greens tend to lose intensity, and most reds, pinks and yellows gain. But you can retain and inject more colour into a room by altering the strength or actual colour of light bulbs. Pink bulbs will shed a softer pink glow, and white bulbs a clean yellow light. Fluorescent lights nearly always look cold and slightly blue, though you can buy a 'warm' var-

iety. They are best limited to lighting kitchen work-tops and concealed in cloakrooms or workshops. Changing the colour of lampshades, from white to rusty red or pink, will also alter the colours shed. And if you spotlight a brightly coloured wall or picture, the colour of the object will be accentuated and bounced off onto other surfaces. For example, a table lamp or spotlight directed onto a bowl of yellow flowers will amplify the yellow in the room.

If when the paint has dried and the curtains are hung you feel a satisfied glow of success, but with hindsight certain aspects of the room do not appear to have gone as you had intended, all is not lost. Small accessories, such as table-cloths, cushions and china, can redress a colour balance and inject extra character. For instance, in a dining-room which turns out rather too blue, a group of yellow pots and lamp-shades can make all the difference.

Designers often recommend that you live with a newly decorated room before you make any extra additions. Personally I think it best to act quickly before your eye becomes used to the way it is. However, like many aspects of interior design there are many schools of thought, which makes decorating such an all-absorbing hobby with infinite possibilities and promise.

A favourite possession – an antique piece of furniture or as in this case a rug – can provide the key to the style and colour scheme of a room. Dark olive green serves to dramatize the rug and draw the eye towards it. The sharp terracotta of the flowers is repeated in the choice of fabric in the Austrian blind and in the footstool.

SOFTENING THE BARE BONES

1

Fabric is wonderful for softening and disguising bumpy walls and ceilings, applied flat with battens and braids, or gathered for extra lushness. Polished wooden floors make the perfect background for puff-quilted and braided rugs, perhaps finished off with a painted stencilled border. Even cupboard panels can be softened with a fabric infill.

TENTED CEILING

This ceiling treatment never fails to win a round of applause. It creates a rather exotic and stunning atmosphere which, combined with a feeling of cosiness, makes it ideal in a dining or sleeping area. It can hide a badly plastered ceiling too. Choose a cheerful fabric to give the room a sense of fun.

This project looks more complicated than it really is. The actual sewing involved is simple machining. The most difficult task is the installation. You will need to enlist the help of several tall friends with steady hands and good balance, and have sturdy chairs or planks and ladders on hand for when you tack or staple the fabric around the room to the pre-erected battens.

You will need a fabric that looks as good gathered as it does laid flat. A glazed chintz would be wonderful, though rather expensive. You will also need 1 × ½in (25 × 12mm) wooden battens to fit around the room, screws and wall plugs, two 12in (30cm) diameter circles cut from plywood or chipboard, tacks, glue, braid and tape.

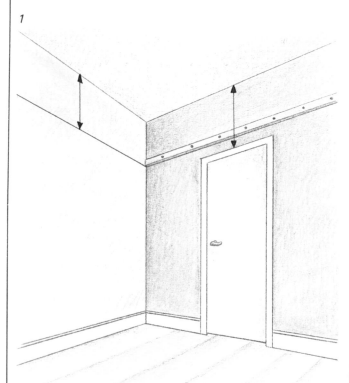

1

Decide on the position for the lower edge of your tent and mark a straight and level line all around the room: about 12in (30cm) down from the ceiling is usually ideal, perhaps less in a small room. Ensure that the line is above the top of any windows and doors in the room (1). Cut lengths of 1 × ½in (25 × 12mm) wooden battens to fit around the room and secure them on the wall. The lower edge of the batten should lie on the marked line. The battens should be firmly secured with wall plugs and screws.

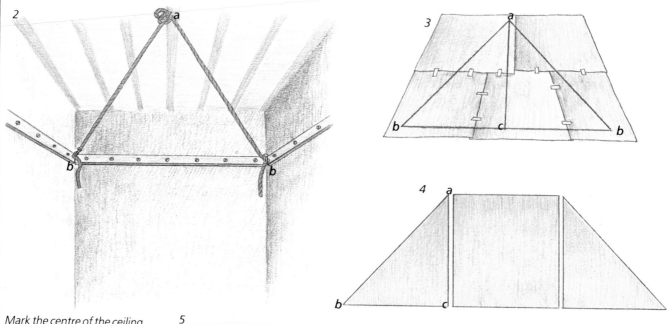

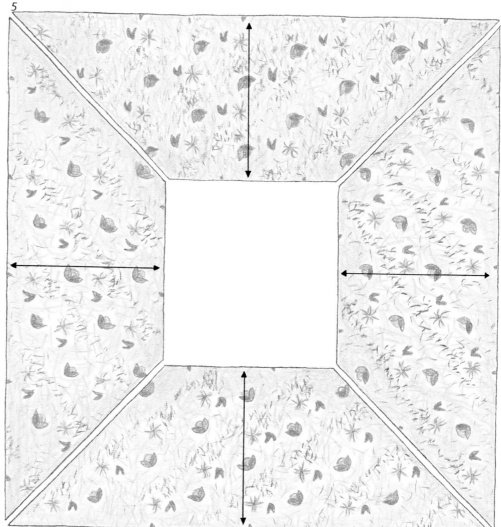

Mark the centre of the ceiling, (make sure there is a joist there), and use two pieces of string to measure from the centre point to the corners of the room at the lower edge of the batten *(2)*.

To make the paper pattern, join sheets of newspaper or tissue paper together. Mark out the triange **abb.** Divide the line **bb** in half, giving point **c** *(3)*. Join **ac** and cut along this line.

With another piece of paper, measure out a rectangle **ac** long by **bc** wide and insert it between the two triangles **abc** *(4)*. This gives you the pattern for one wall. Repeat for the other three walls if your room is not square.

With the pattern as a guide, cut out the fabric, sewing together sufficient widths of fabric to make up the tent. Add 3in (8cm) all around the inner and outer edges for the casing and ruffle. The grain of the fabric should run from the outside to the centre of the tent *(5)*. Sew the pieces together with flat seams and press open. It is advisable to pink the seams (see page 178) to avoid any fraying when the tent is cleaned.

6

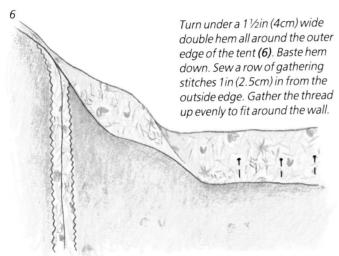

Turn under a 1½in (4cm) wide double hem all around the outer edge of the tent (6). Baste hem down. Sew a row of gathering stitches 1in (2.5cm) in from the outside edge. Gather the thread up evenly to fit around the wall.

7

Pin and stitch the gathered edge onto a piece of tape to hold the gathers evenly (7).

8

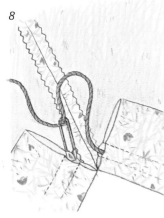

Turn under a ¼in (6mm) hem and then a 1in (2.5cm) hem around the inner edge of the tent. Hem and make a casing ¼in (6mm) wide close to the hemmed edge. Thread a length of cord through the casing (8).

Cut a circle 12in (30cm) in diameter out of chipboard or plywood. Put it on a piece of the fabric and mark a circle. Cut out the circle allowing 6in (15cm) all around. Glue the fabric to one side of the wooden circle, taking it over to the other side. Secure it firmly (9).

9

Secure another wooden circle of the same size to the centre of the ceiling, screwing it firmly to a joist (10). If you have a central light fitting you can achieve the same effect by cutting rings of wood. Check the position of the wiring before screwing to the ceiling.

Staple or tack the taped outer edge of the fabric to the lower edge of the batten, leaving a ruffle hanging down (11). Cover the line of tacks with braid if necessary.

12

Take the fabric-covered circle and screw or nail it fabric-side down onto the first plate, sandwiching the fullness of the fabric between the two. Make a 2in (5cm) wide double ribbon of fabric, 1½ times the circumference of the circle. Pleat it onto the edges of the wood and secure with tacks (13). Glue braid over tacks.

10

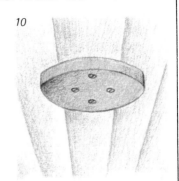

11

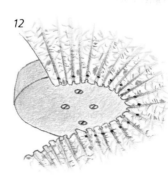

The illustration above is to show how the fabric drapes. The fabric is easier to fix if someone supports the bulk of it as it is tacked or stapled. After the outer edge is fixed, draw up the fullness and adjust the tautness of the tent as you work. Tack or staple the inner gathered edge to the wooden circle at the centre of the room (12).

13

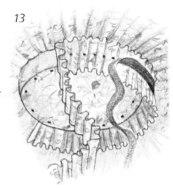

FABRIC-COVERED WALLS

Fabric wall covering is luxurious and it is also an effective way to hide badly plastered walls. This is an expensive idea, however, but the results are sumptuous. Wire or metal stays, which hold the fabric lengths at the top and bottom, make it easy to take the fabric down and clean it, and there are other practical advantages too. The fabric acts as sound-proofing and it makes the room warmer and cosier. As well as your chosen fabric, you will need 1 × ½in (25 × 12mm) wooden battens to go around the room top and bottom, screws and wall plugs, curtain wire or rods and screw eyes.

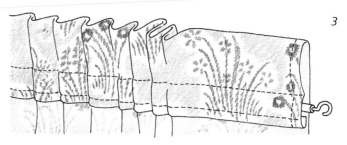

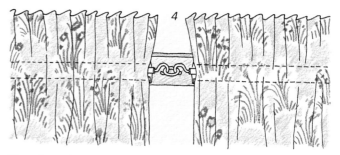

Turn under and stitch a ½in (12mm) double hem down the sides of all fabric sections. Turn under ½in (12mm) and then 1½in (4cm) all along the top and bottom edges. Pin and baste, then sew two lines of stitching to make a ½in (12mm) casing ¾in (2cm) from the fold at the outer edge (3).

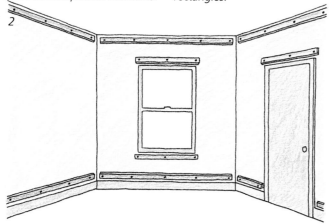

Thread curtain wires through the casings. Turn the screw eyes to a horizontal position and fit the curtain wires through them to hang the rectangles of fabric (4). Distribute the fullness of the fabric evenly along each wire, drawing the ends of the fabric casing over each hook to hide it.

Fit all the other panels round the room, including the sections above and below the windows (5).

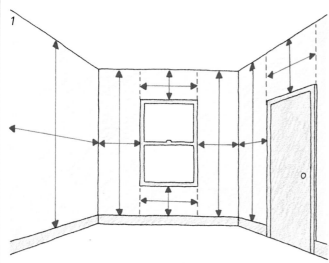

Divide the room into rectangular sections: whole walls, alcoves, areas above doors and windows (1). Measure each section. Cut fabric into pieces for each section, 1½ times the width of the rectangles, plus 4in (10cm) for the top and bottom hems. Add 2in (5cm) for side hems. Join fabric strips with flat seams.

Screw lengths of 1 × ½in (25 × 12mm) wooden batten to the wall all around the top and bottom of the room and above the doors and above and below the windows (2). Fit screw eyes to the front edge of the battens at each end and at intermediate points where necessary to correspond with the measured rectangles.

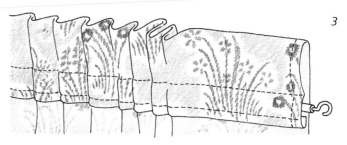

WALL HANGING

An interesting piece of fabric makes a wonderful wall hanging. This one is quilted along the stripes of the pattern and bound on all sides. It is then hung from loops slid onto a decorative pole which is secured to the wall just below the ceiling. By choosing such a colourful and varied pattern in the fabric, the wall hanging looks like a patchwork as well as a quilt. For a wall hanging approximately 6 × 7ft (1.8 × 2.1 metres), you will need 6 yards (5.4 metres) each of fabric, wadding and muslin for the backing, strong cotton for the loops and the top facing, and a decorative pole.

Decide on the dimensions of your hanging. This one is made up of two 36in (91cm) wide strips with bound edges and a central strip (1). Cut the two main panels 84in (213cm) long. Then cut two side binding pieces 6 × 84in (15 × 213cm); a top strip 3 × 80in (8 × 233cm), a bottom strip 10 × 80in (25 × 233cm), two central strips 3 × 84in (8 × 233cm), and five strips 8 × 9in (20 × 23cm) for the hanging loops.

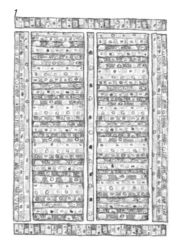

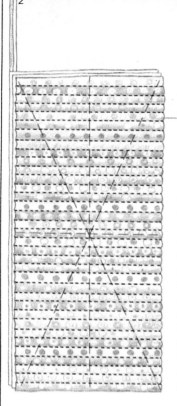

For the backing you will need two pieces of muslin and wadding cut to the same size as the panels. Lay out one piece of muslin, wadding and fabric, right sides up, raw edges together. Pin and baste around all layers (2). Repeat with the second panel. Now quilt the panels using a straight machine stitch. Work from the right side and follow the lines of the pattern. If you are quilting the outline of a motif, rather than a geometric pattern, stitch the layers together around the edges as well. Remove basting stitches.

Lap one panel 2 in (5cm) over the other and stitch together down both raw edges. Take one centre strip, turn under ½in (12mm) down both sides and pin over the join. Repeat on wrong side with the other strip. Machine stitch through all layers (3). Pin side binding to hanging, right sides facing. Stitch ½in (12mm) from raw edges (4). Press binding towards seam allowance. Cut 2½in (7cm) strip of wadding and place it over the seam allowance and baste to the binding. Turn under the raw edge of the binding and

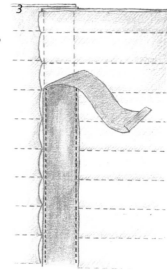

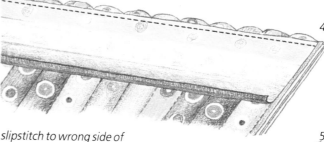

slipstitch to wrong side of hanging, enclosing wadding. Repeat for other side. Make five hanging loops from the strips. Pin to right side of hanging at top at equal intervals (5). Turn under ¼in (6mm) all

around the top strip. Pin with right side facing to hanging (5) enclosing loops. Stitch and turn to wrong side. Hem down sides and across the bottom. Quilt the bottom strip and position it across the lower edge, right sides facing. Stitch and turn under a ½in (12mm) hem along the other edge. Fold bottom strip in half, slipstitch hemmed edge to wrong side of hanging. Turn in ends and slipstitch closed (6).

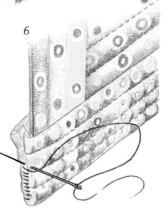

Collecting small pieces of fabric to make into patchwork appeals to the squirrel instinct in most of us, but the daunting task of cutting and sewing together hundreds of tiny geometric shapes deters all but the most committed. The joy of this cotton quilted rug design is that although it looks complicated, it is incredibly simple to make. Also it is soft under foot, machine washable, and an ideal buffer for a child's room. The rug is 40in (102cm) square, and is made of four separate patches, each consisting of four 20½ × 5½in (52 × 14cm) strips. For the backing you need a plain piece of fabric 40in (102cm) square, and for the quilting about 2 yards (2 metres) of medium weight wadding. Prepare to make the rug by cutting out 16 strips in two or three different fabrics; woven cotton of the same weight would be ideal.

4

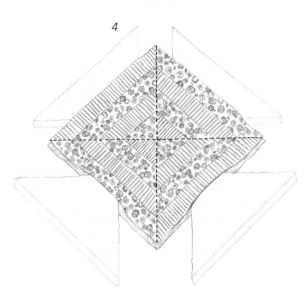

1

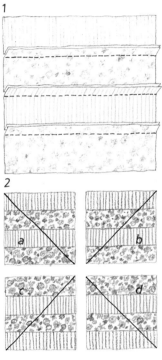

2

3

Make up the squares, pinning and sewing together your prepared strips, right sides facing, in this order: a strip of blue and white stripe, a small floral print, followed by a strip of pink and white striped fabric, ending with a strip of the same floral (1). Press all seams open. Place the squares right side up on the floor with the blue stripe patches lying on the outer edges (2). Now cut the squares across the diagonal lines as indicated to make eight triangles. Exchange piece a with b and c with d to make up the finished pattern (3). Once rearranged, pin, baste and stitch the pieces, right sides facing, to make up four squares again. Now stitch them together and press seams open.

To quilt the rug, cut out a piece of backing fabric to the same size and lay it down with the wrong side uppermost. Lay the patchwork piece right side up on top of it. Pin the two pieces together along the diagonal lines of seaming. Baste and machine stitch them together following the diagonal lines as accurately as possible. Now cut out four triangular pieces of wadding to stuff the rug (4). Make sure the whole of each triangle is well padded and then pin the wadding in place along

the square seam lines. Machine stitch the innermost square along seam line (5). Continue this process until each square has been sewn in place (6).

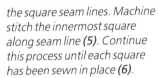

5

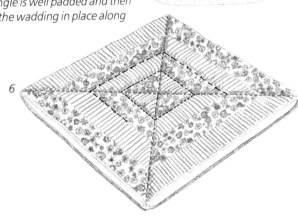

6

To finish off, cut 3in (8cm) wide strips of pink and white striped fabric to make up four 41½in (105cm) lengths. With wrong sides facing, turn in two ¼in (6mm) hems along each edge and then fold the whole strip in half. Press. Fold this trim over

the raw edges of the rug to enclose them, pin and baste. Turn in and baste at the corners or mitre them (see page 178). Slipstitch the corners and machine stitch the edging in place all around.

BRAIDED RUG

Braided rugs are a good way to inject colour into a room. This design is made up from rolls of kitchen cleaning cloths, but it can be made with any knitted or woven fabric made up into strips. You will need dyes and, depending on the size of your rug, you will need strips of fabric 3½ times the length of all the braids. For example, this 4ft (122cm) long rug has 12 lengths of braid: so 4ft (122cm) × 12 × 3½ = 168ft (1708cm) of fabric strips.

Before stitching, the cotton cloths must be washed to shrink the fabric and dyed to change the neutral colour into different hues. The washing removes any dressing from the fabric, preparing it for the dyeing process. The easiest way to do this is in one step in the washing machine for each colour. After dyeing, roll up each length of cotton into strips about 1in (2.5cm) wide **(1)**. With a matching thread, hand stitch down the raw edges to keep the strip from unwinding **(2)**. Work with neat straight stitches across the raw edge. Stitch each length in the same way. If you want to braid your rug with a woven fabric, cut strips 2¼in

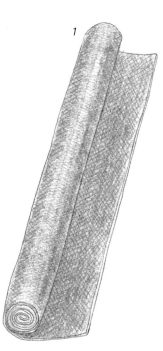

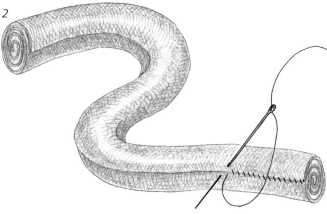

(6cm) wide and turn them in along the raw edges for ¼in (6mm) and then fold each strip in half and press. There is no need to sew the strips together lengthwise. It is better to cut woven fabrics on the bias, this makes the braids more flexible to work with. Make sure all the

strips for braiding are the same thickness, otherwise the finished rug will wear unevenly. Choose contrasting colours in your fabrics; you can even use three different fabrics together in the same braid.

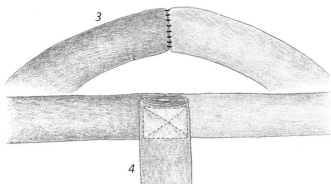

Take two strips and with seams at the back, stitch the ends together (3). Machine stitch the third strip centrally over the join (4).

Weave the strips together in a three-strand braid, always positioning the seams at the back (5). Try to join in new lengths of fabric at different positions so that the joins can be staggered. Join the strips together (3) and then push the seam inside the weaving to hide the join (6).

When each braid measures the required length of the rug, place the braids side by side on a flat surface, and using a double thread take a stitch through each braid in turn (7). Pull up the threads so that the braids lie firmly together. Tuck the ends under one another to make a neat edge and stitch firmly to hold.

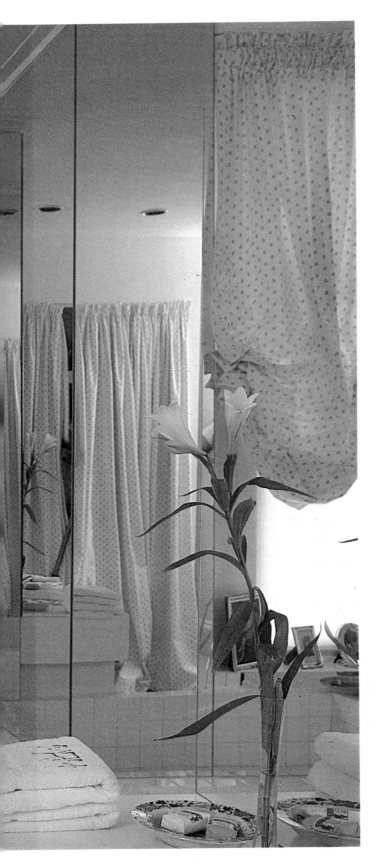

2

WINDOW DRESSING

As well as creating a style, it is easy to change the proportions of your windows by the way you dress them. To make a narrow window seem wider, extend your track or curtain rod beyond the frame, so that the curtains hang outside the window frame instead of overlapping it. To heighten a window, position a pelmet or the curtain itself some distance above the top of the frame, tie the curtain gathers together so they meet at the top, and scoop them back at the sides with tie-backs. If you are lucky enough to have a window which is architecturally unusual, emphasize its shape with a blind, recessed inside the window frame so as not to obscure it.

UNLINED CURTAINS

Unlined curtains are a perfect project for beginners and they should not be shrugged off as a second best to lined curtains (see overleaf); at certain windows they may be a more sensible choice. For example, in a kitchen there may be less room on either side of the window and cooking steam means they will need frequent washing. Problems only arise with windows wide enough to need more than one fabric width; most curtains look better if the seams don't show.

Here the sheer curtain acts as a soft lightscreen and the seams are not so apparent. The tie-backs and the edge of the sheer curtain are finished in the matching border cut from the curtain fabric. You will need curtain fabric – for this project choose one with a border design – heading tape, a decorative pole and rings, weights to help the curtains hang well, a sheer fabric, covered curtain wire or a curtain rod, hooks and rings to secure the tie-backs.

Fix up the curtain pole and the fittings for the sheer curtains and measure the window for the curtains (see page 180). Cut out as many fabric widths as you need. Cut the selvedges from all fabric lengths. Pin and stitch

lengths together with flat fell seams (1). If you don't want to remove the selvedges, you can cut notches in the selvedge at regular intervals of about 4-6in (10-15cm).

Fasten hooks through heading tape and hang curtain from pole. Hold back the curtain with a tape measure to determine the length for the tie-back (5). Decide on the width. Cut two pieces of fabric and one of interfacing for each tie-back (6). Iron interfacing to wrong side of one piece of fabric. Right sides facing, stitch around all sides leaving an opening to turn out (7). Trim and turn out. Slipstitch closed and attach rings (8) to either end.

1

2

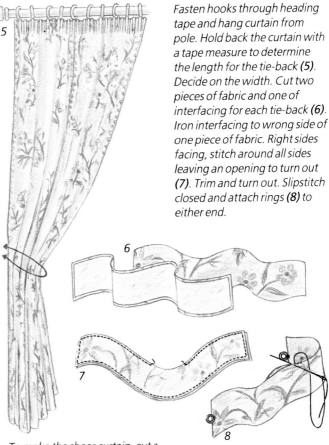

5

Pin a double 1in (2.5cm) hem down both sides of each curtain. Pin a double 2in (5cm) hem along the bottom edge. Mitre the bottom corners (see page 179). Stitch a weight into the corner behind the hem. Slipstitch across the mitred corner. Slipstitch all the hems, adding weights inside the hem at the base of every seam line (2). Make sure the top edge is straight. Position heading tape wrong side facing the right side of the curtain, overlap them ¼in (6mm) and leave ½in (12mm) of tape free at either end. Pin and stitch the heading tape (3). Turn to wrong side of

fabric and pin and stitch along bottom of tape (4). Leaving cords free at outside edges, turn under a hem and stitch the ends of tape. Pull up cords to correct width for the window. Tie together, do not cut.

To make the sheer curtain, cut a length of fabric to size, up to 1½ times the width of the window. Pin and stitch a double ½in (12mm) hem down both sides (9). Turn under top edge ½in (12mm) and then 3in

6

7

8

(8cm). Pin and stitch close to hem line. Stitch a further row 1in (2.5cm) above the previous row to form a casing. Thread a covered wire or a curtain rod through the casing (10).

3

4

9

10

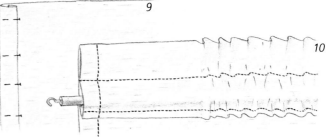

Make up a border the width of the sheer curtain plus a ½in (12mm) allowance all around. Turn under this allowance all around the border. Press. Turn up ½in (12mm) hem to right side of curtain. Position fabric strip to base edge of curtain (11). Pin and topstitch.

11

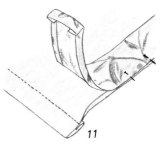

LINED CURTAINS

With a lining curtains hang better and, if full length, they increase the apparent height of a room. Consider all the various headings available; they should complement the style of the room. First you must decide on your heading tape – here triple pleats fall in gracefully with the English decorator style. You will need enough fabric to cover the width of the window the number of times necessary for the heading tape, curtain track, weights, lining fabric and hooks and screw eyes to anchor the curtains.

Measure your windows (see page 180) and fix the curtain track in place. Decide on the length of your curtains and choose a curtain heading tape. This will dictate the fullness of the curtains. Here, the curtains are hung from a tape that has cords running through it which draw the heading into triple pinched pleats. The top of the curtain is flush with the top of the track. The finished width of these curtains is twice the width of the area they cover when they are drawn closed. Add 1½in (4cm) for side hems. Add 2in (5cm) for the bottom hem and 3in (8cm) for the top. If fabric widths need to be joined, allow ½in (12mm) for seams. Calculate how many widths of fabric you will need, making allowances if you choose a pattern. Cut out fabric for curtains and join widths and part widths for each curtain with flat seams (1).

1

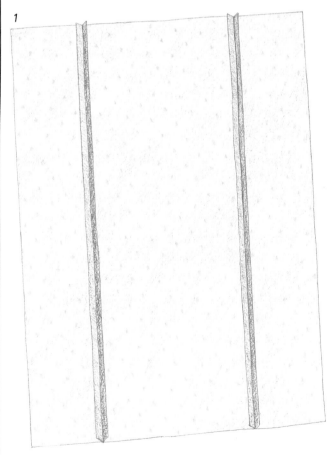

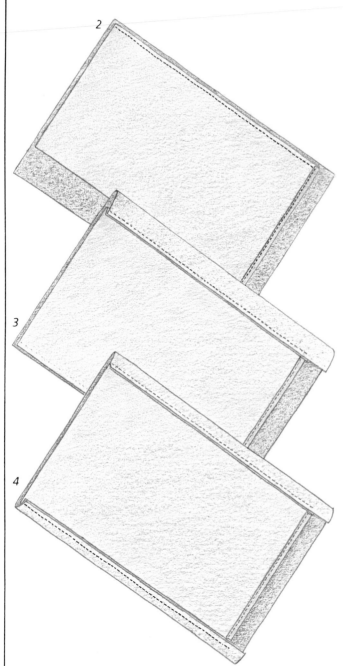

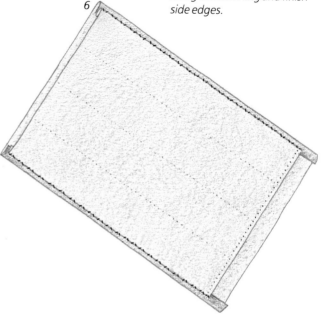

For a locked-in lining, cut the lining as for loose lining **(2-4)** and hem bottom edge. Turn under and press 1½in (4cm) down each side of curtain fabric. Lay lining over curtain, wrong sides facing, with raw edges of lining matching the folded sides of the curtain. Use a loose lock stitch (see page 176) to join lining to curtain. Make rows of stitches about 20in (51cm) apart across the width of the curtain **(5)**. Start by locking in the lining down the centre of the curtain and work outwards. Turn under and pin a ¾in (2cm) hem down each side of lining. Slipstitch fold of lining to curtain fabric on hem allowance **(6)**. Note: For extra insulation, you can interline the curtains. Use a soft, fairly thick fabric, such as flannelette. Cut interlining the same size as the lining and lock it into the curtain as above. Lock lining to interlining and finish side edges.

For a loose lining, make up the lining panels the same width and the same length as the finished curtain. Turn up and stitch a ½in (12mm) single hem across the lower edge of curtain lining. With right sides facing, pin and stitch one side of curtain and lining together **(2)**. The bottom of the lining should be 3in (8cm) from the bottom edge of the curtain. Adjust position of lining so that other edge of curtain and lining can be pinned and stitched **(3)**. Centre lining on the curtain **(4)** and press seams towards the centre of the curtain. Turn right side out and press to make crisp creases down each side, first centring the lining so that the curtain turnings on each side are of equal width.

The next step is to attach the heading tape to the curtain. Cut the tape the width of the flat curtain, plus ¾ (2cm) at each end. If using a corded tape, cut the tape so that you have a flat section at the centre of the curtains.

If using pocketed heading tape, work out the positions of the pleats on the track (7), ensuring that they are evenly spaced, that the fullness of the fabric will all be taken up, and that there are no pleats at the edges of the curtain.

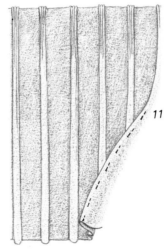

Turn under ½in (12mm) then 2in (5cm) across the top of the curtain. Press. Position curtain tape over folded edge of the curtain fabric close to the top of the curtain. Turn under ¾ (2cm) at each end of tape. Pin and stitch tape, being careful not to stitch across the pockets and the cords at either end. Insert hooks (8) and check that the curtain fits the track, with the pleats evenly spaced. Press curtain well, but do not press pleats.

For detachable linings, the lining is made up separately and attached to the curtain with a special heading tape. Cut the curtain fabric as before. Turn under ½in (12mm) and the 1in (2.5cm) down each side of curtain. Pin and slipstitch. Attach heading tape. Cut the lining the same width as the finished curtain and 1½in (4cm) shorter. Turn under and stitch a ½in (12mm) double hem down both sides and across the lower edge. Insert the raw top edge of

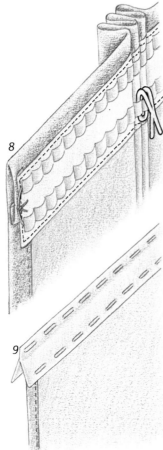

the lining into the fold of the detachable lining tape (9). Stitch tape to lining along bottom edge.

For a professional finish, it is a good idea to 'set' the pleats. Use basting stitches to set the pleats together at the top (10).

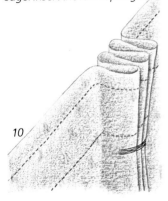

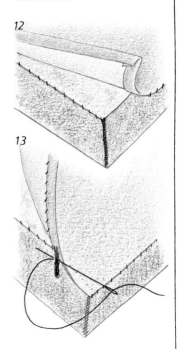

Unpick the side hems on the lining for about 2in (5cm) at the lower edge. Turn up the curtain hem along the line of pins and trim away excess fabric at corners. Mitre the corners neatly (see page 179), slipstitching the folded edges together by hand (12). Hem stitch the lower edge of the curtain and re-stitch the lining at the bottom corners.

To hold the lining hem to the curtain make bar tacks at 20in (51cm) intervals across the width of the curtain. Take four or five ½in (12mm) wide loose stitches from the hem of the curtain to the hem of the lining. Make buttonhole stitches (see page 176) over the threads to give a secure bar (13). Do not stitch through to the right side of the curtain.

With full, tied-back curtains, it is advisable to anchor the outer corners of the curtains so they

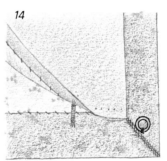

Hang the curtains from the track and pin the pleats all down the length of the curtain (11). Leave the curtains to hang for about 12-14 days. Remove the pins and basting and leave the curtains to hang while you take up the hem. Mark the position of the fold of the hem at floor level with a line of pins. If the lower edge of the curtain has become crushed through lying on the floor, press it. Turn under and press a 1in (2.5cm) single hem across the bottom edge of the curtain.

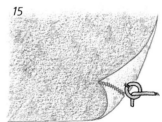

hang crisply. Stitch a small ring to the hem at the bottom outer corner of each curtain (14). Fix a hook to the skirting board, level with the ring and directly below the ends of the curtain track. Slip hook over ring (15) to hold curtain taut.

This window treatment where the denser fabric is used for the blind and the sheer for the curtains is an unusual one. The blind does the practical job of keeping out light and the sheer curtains provide a delicate, decorative prettiness. You will need a roller blind kit, tacks, cord, a curtain rod, rings and screw eyes for the tie-backs, sufficient fabric for your windows and aerosol fabric stiffener. If you buy special roller blind fabric, it is not necessary to hem the sides; use scotch tape to hold any hems in place as the pin holes may remain.

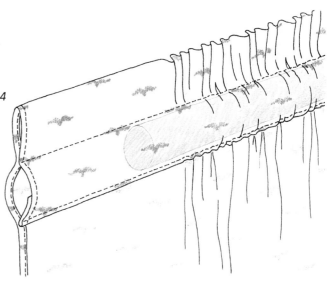

Measure up for the roller blind (see page 180). Fasten the brackets at the window with the pin hole on the right-hand side. Following the manufacturer's instructions, cut the roller to fit the brackets and fit pin and cap in place. Cut fabric to correct size adding ½in (12mm) for side seams and 2in (5cm) for the

batten casing. Turn in ¼in (6mm) side hems and zigzag stitch over the raw edges. For the casing, turn up ½in (12mm) and then 1½in (4cm).

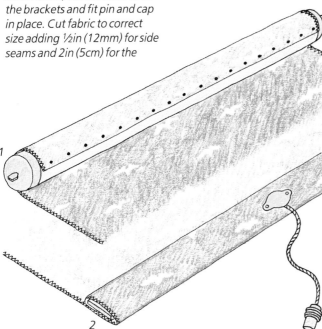

Measure the window for curtains (see page 180) and cut out sufficient fabric widths for each curtain. Remove selvedges from each fabric width and join any seams with a flat fell seam. On each curtain turn under a double ½in (12mm) hem at side edges. Pin and stitch. Turn under ½in (12mm) and then a further 3½in (9cm) along the top edge. Pin and stitch hem and then sew another row 1½in (4cm) above first row to form a casing. Thread curtain rod through the casing,

gathering up the top edge to form a ruffle (4). Hang the curtain and decide on the length. Hem the bottom edge of the curtain with a special foot on the sewing machine (5) or roll and slipstitch in place by hand.

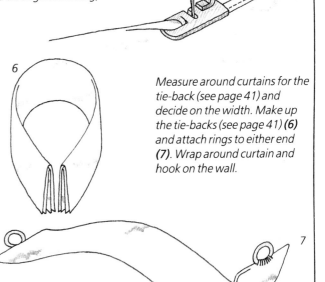

Pin and stitch hem and one side of casing. To attach the fabric to the roller, turn the fabric ½in (12mm) to the right side along the raw edge and butt up to the straight line on the roller. Tack in place (1). Stiffen fabric (see

page 148). Cut batten to length and slot into casing; stitch casing closed (2). Thread a cord through the holder and acorn and screw the holder to the batten through fabric casing at back of blind. Hang blind (3).

Measure around curtains for the tie-back (see page 41) and decide on the width. Make up the tie-backs (see page 41) (6) and attach rings to either end (7). Wrap around curtain and hook on the wall.

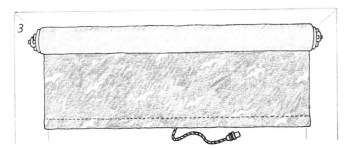

APPLIQUÉD ROLLER BLIND

Successful appliqué work requires careful planning and mixing of the right fabrics and colours. Most of this design is confined to the bottom edge to avoid making the blind too bulky. You will need a light cotton fabric for the blind or special roller blind fabric, a roller blind kit, glue or scotch tape, a wooden batten, cord and an aerosol fabric stiffener.

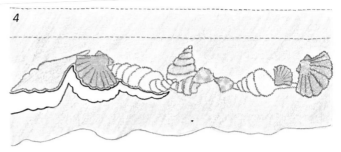

Fix up brackets (see pages 46-47) at the window. Cut the roller to fit and measure it to determine the width of the blind plus ½in (12mm) either side for hems. Turn in side edges and press. Pin and zigzag stitch over raw edges down each side.

Turn up lower edge ½in (12mm) and then 8in (20cm). Pin and stitch along folded ege (1). Stitch another row 1½in (4cm) from the first to form a casing for the batten (2). Slipstitch across one end of casing.

Pull any loose threads to the wrong side and thread them back into the stitching. With a pair of sharp embroidery scissors, carefully cut away the allowance around the top of the motifs close to the stitching and then cut around the motifs at the bottom of the blind through

all layers (4). Add individual motifs to the remainder of the blind in the same way. If you have used regular fabric, stiffen the whole blind with a stiffener, following the manufacturer's instructions. Cut a wooden batten ½in (12mm) shorter than the batten casing.

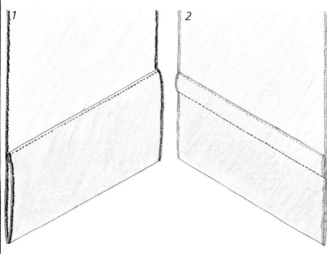

Work out appliqué design and make a paper pattern for each motif (see page 166). Cut out the motifs from different coloured fabrics allowing ¼-½in (6-12mm) all around. Draw in internal lines. Position the

motifs near the base edge of the blind, butting and overlapping them until you get the desired effect. Pin and baste around each motif. Zigzag stitch around each motif (3), stitching any internal design lines.

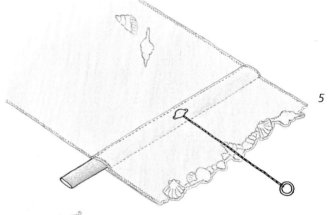

Insert batten into casing and slipstitch closed. Thread one end of cord through holder and knot. Thread other end through a ring and knot to the required length. Screw holder into batten at back of casing (5). Make sure that the top edge of the blind is straight, turn under ½in (12mm) and press. Spread a thin layer of glue along the line on the roller and press the folded edge over it. (Alternatively, you can hold it in place with scotch tape). Tack in place, beginning at the centre and working out towards each end (6), spacing tacks about ¾in (2cm) apart. Hand roll the blind to achieve the correct tension and position it between the brackets.

ROMAN BLINDS

For a tailored and elegant style of window dressing, Roman blinds are the obvious choice. You should use a closely woven fabric. Unless your window is exceptionally wide you can avoid joins. Choose a striped fabric or a plain-coloured chintz with a woven stripe – the job of sewing on the vertical tapes will be that much easier.

You need enough fabric to cover your windows plus seam allowances. To draw the blind up in horizontal folds you need to sew tapes and rings to the back. You also need cord, screw eyes, a cleat and a heading board held by angle irons.

1

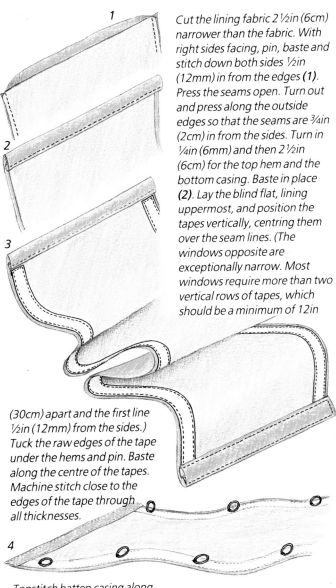

Cut the lining fabric 2½in (6cm) narrower than the fabric. With right sides facing, pin, baste and stitch down both sides ½in (12mm) in from the edges (**1**). Press the seams open. Turn out and press along the outside edges so that the seams are ¾in (2cm) in from the sides. Turn in ¼in (6mm) and then 2½in (6cm) for the top hem and the bottom casing. Baste in place (**2**). Lay the blind flat, lining uppermost, and position the tapes vertically, centring them over the seam lines. (The windows opposite are exceptionally narrow. Most windows require more than two vertical rows of tapes, which should be a minimum of 12in

2

3

(30cm) apart and the first line ½in (12mm) from the sides.) Tuck the raw edges of the tape under the hems and pin. Baste along the centre of the tapes. Machine stitch close to the edges of the tape through all thicknesses.

4

Topstitch batten casing along three sides, leaving an opening for the batten (**3**). Mark the position of the rings with pins, placing the first ring 4in (10cm) above the batten casing, and the last 6in (15cm) below the top hem. Space the remaining four rings at equal intervals down both sides, making sure the positions correspond exactly 6in (15cm) apart. Sew the rings in place by hand, attaching them to the tape only so that the stitches do not show through onto the blind (**4**). Slot the batten through the casing and slipstitch closed (**5**).

5

6

Prepare the wooden heading board by screwing eyes to the underside, lining them up with the top rings. Screw angle irons to the inside edge of the board where it will butt up to the window (**6**).

7

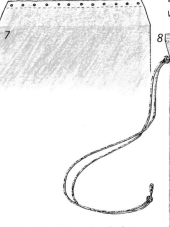

8

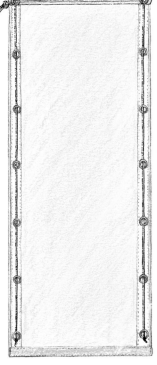

Using ½in (12mm) upholstery tacks spaced 1in (2.5cm) apart, tack the blind to the heading board (**7**). Cut two pieces of cord — one equal to twice the length of one tape plus the width of the blind, the other twice the length of the tape only. With the right side down, lay the blind flat and knot the cords to the bottom rings, keeping the shorter piece on the side that will be anchored to the window's edge.

9

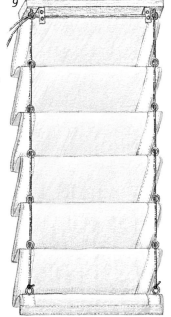

Thread the cords up through the rings and through the screw eyes, carrying the longer cord along the top. Knot the cords together 1in (2.5cm) from the last screw eye (**8**). Trim the bottom ends level with the bottom of the blind and knot together.

Mount the heading board by screwing the angle irons to the window (**9**). Attach a cleat to the edge of the window or to the wall and wind the cords around it to anchor the blind. Clean the fabric regularly by removing dust from the folds.

AUSTRIAN BLINDS

Austrian blinds are made in the same way as Roman blinds but the top is gathered and the bottom edge folds into soft, curved swags. The bottom edges are usually finished off with a ruffle or decorative lace. Austrian blinds are not always lined, but if they are, the lining should be attached to the blind before any tapes are sewn on. Then the lining and the fabric are treated as one piece of cloth. You will need enough fabric to cover the width of the window 2¼ times, Austrian blind tape, decorative lace, curtain heading tape, a headboard and angle irons, two pulleys, screw eyes, cleats and cord to pull the blinds up.

Turn under ½in (12mm) and then 1½in (4cm) across the top of the blind. Position pencil pleating heading tape over the hem on the wrong side of the blind (3). Pin and stitch in place, turning under raw edges. The ends of the Austrian blind tape will now be enclosed in the top and bottom hems. These tapes do not pull up; the cord running through them forms loops to carry the draw cords.

1 intervals across the blind (1). Stitch in place down edges of tape. Turn up and stitch a ½in (12mm) double hem at the lower edge of the blind. Cut a length of 5-6in (12-15cm) wide scalloped lace to fit across the bottom. Stitch a narrow rolled hem at each short end of the lace and pin the straight edge over the hem of the blind. Zigzag stitch lace in place (2). Fix the heading board above the window with angle irons (see page 51).

Measure the window (see page 180) and cut the fabric 2¼ times the width of the finished blind plus 1½in (4cm) side hem allowance. Add 2in (5cm) for the top and bottom hems. Turn under ¾in (2cm) down each edge and pin special Austrian blind tape over the edge of the turning (see page 51 for position of loops). Pin additional lengths of tape at 12in (30cm)

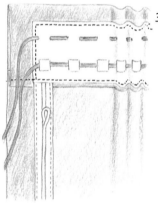

Fix screw eyes to the front of the board every 4-6in (10-15cm). Draw up the heading tape to match the length of the board. Fit hooks on the heading tape and hang them from the screw eyes. Fix large screw eyes to the underside of the heading board at the top of every vertical tape. Fix the pulleys to each end of the heading board (4). Thread the cords through the loops, screw eyes and pulleys (see page 54).

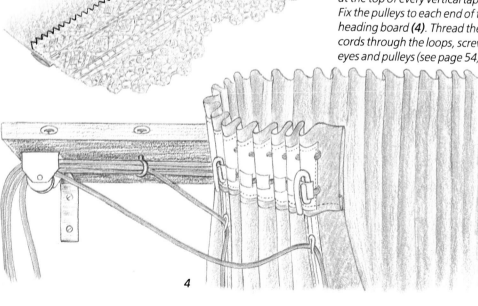

BALLOON BLINDS

Balloon blinds are similar to Austrian blinds except the gathering lines are positioned at either end and the bottom edge is shaped in a semi-circle so they look more like a flexible pelmet than a blind. They look elegant in a row of two or three as here where the blinds correspond to the positions of the window mullions on the large modern window. You will need a lightweight curtain fabric, pencil pleating heading tape, Austrian blind tape, cord, pulleys, angle irons, a heading board and screw eyes.

The balloon blind hangs from a heading board fixed above the window with angle irons (1). You then need to fix a curtain track to the front of the board, a pulley at either end and screw eyes to the lower side of the board. These screw eyes carry the cords and need to be spaced evenly across the board, about 6in (15cm) apart.

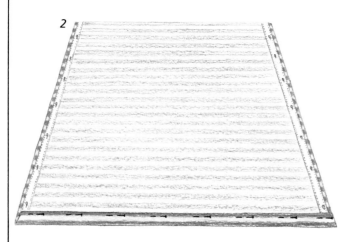

Cut the fabric twice the width of the track plus 2in (5cm) side hem allowance. The length should be equal to the finished length of the blind plus 4in (10cm) allowance. Turn in 1in (2.5cm) down each side and baste. Cover the raw edge with Austrian blind tape (see pages 52-53). Pin in place and machine stitch down each edge of the tape. Turn up ½in (12mm) and then 1½in (4cm) across the lower edge. Pin and hem stitch (2). Turn under ½in (12mm) and 1½in (4cm) at the top edge of the blind. Pin and baste.

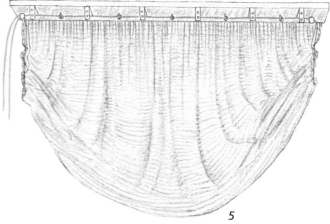

Pin pencil pleating tape to the top of the blind ¼in (6mm) below the folded top of the blind. Turn under ½in (12mm) at each end of tape. Stitch tape on all sides, covering the raw edge of the hem and leaving the ends of the cords which run through the tape free (3).

Draw up the cords so the blind fits the track. Fit hooks into the tape, positioning them so that the heading covers the track once the blind is hung. Cut two lengths of cord; one piece 1½ times the length of the blind, the other 1½ times the length plus the width of the blind.

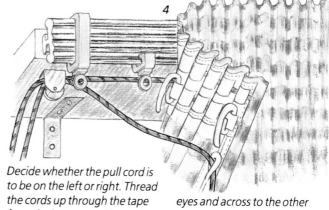

Decide whether the pull cord is to be on the left or right. Thread the cords up through the tape from the bottom and hang the blind (4). Take one cord through the pulley, the screw eyes and across to the other pulley. The other cord just runs through one pulley (5). Fix cleats to the window to hold.

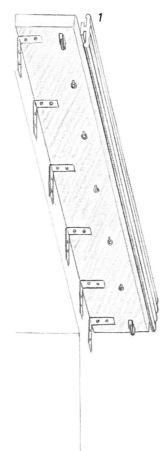

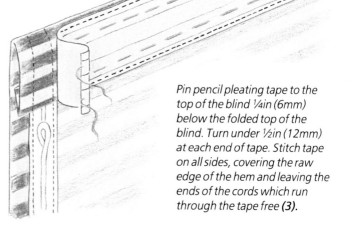

RUFFLED CURTAINS WITH VALANCE

Looking cheerfully extravagant, without involving a fortune spent on fabric, this window treatment is a triumph of prettiness. It combines the use of three different fabrics, the most expensive floral polished cotton is used sparingly, the cheap pink curtain fabric is used for the main curtain widths and a pink taffeta is used for the ruffles along the valance and down the border to tailor the lushness. You will need three curtain fabrics, a decorative pole and rings, gathering heading tape, and a decorative knob or brass rose for either side of the window over which to catch the curtains to hold them back. The rosette tie-back fixings are an important detail, succinctly in keeping with the florid flounciness of the soft romantic style.

The actual design of this window dressing is economic in terms of effort and heading tape. The valance is cut in two pieces, the same width as the curtain, and it is attached to the curtain with the heading tape in the final stages. The curtains are best left unlined as there is a generous amount of fabric and it drapes along the floor too.

Measure the window (see page 180). Each curtain is the width of the window. The length is the distance from the pole to the floor plus 11in (28cm). Cut out two curtain widths, joining seams where necessary, and hem outer edges with ½in (12mm) double-hem.

Decide on the shape of the valance. Cut a template from newspaper; the valance should come about a third of the way down the window and the width should be the same as the curtains. Exaggerate the curve for a good shape.

Cut two strips of floral fabric 12in (30cm) wide, and the length of the curtain. Cut two 4in (10cm) wide strips of pink fabric, 1½ times the length of the floral border piece. Make up ruffle (1). Stitch to right side of one edge of border strip (4). Pin,

baste and stitch other edge of border to outer edge of curtain length, right side of border facing wrong side of curtain (5). Turn border to right side of curtain, press and machine stitch through all layers (6).

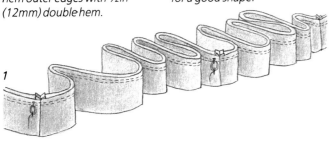

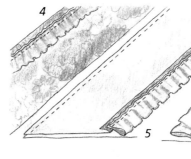

Cut out both sides of the valance and measure down the side and around the shaped edge. Cut strips of pink fabric 10in (25cm) wide to make a strip 1½ times this length. Fold lengthwise, wrong sides facing. Run two lines of gathering stitch through raw edges of ruffle (1). Draw up gathering threads so

ruffle fits down the side and across the shaped edge of the valance. Pin each piece to right side of valance, positioning raw edges 1in (2.5cm) in from the raw edges of the valance. Ruffle should point towards the middle of the valance. Baste and stitch in place (2), distributing fullness evenly.

Turn up ½in (12mm) and 2½in (6cm) along lower edge of curtain. Trim away bulk of ruffle and slipstitch hem in place. Turn ½in (12mm) single hem to right side of curtains along the top edge and press. Turn under ½in (12mm) across top edge of valance to wrong side. Trim away ruffle at top outer edges and neaten. Lay out valance,

wrong side uppermost. Lay curtain on top, right side down, with single hems matching along top edge, leaving ruffle free. Pin and stitch standard heading tape in place 1½in (4cm) from the top (7) through all layers to hold valance and curtain together. Leave cords of

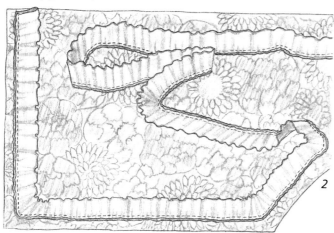

Turn under a ½in (12mm) wide double hem along inside edges of valance. Pin and stitch. Turn under and press a ½in (12mm) single hem down outer edges and across lower edge. Turn this folded edge of valance over trimmed seam allowance of ruffle and pin in place. Stitch close to previous line of stitching (3). Press ruffle outwards.

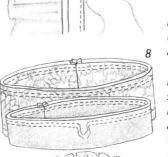

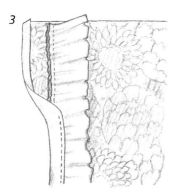

heading tape free and turn under short tape edges. Sew across edges through all layers.

Fit a knob or brass rose to either side of window at the desired height. Cut a 12in (30cm) strip and an 8in (20cm) strip of floral fabric, both 36in (91cm) long. Join ends of each to form rings. Fold in half lengthwise, wrong sides facing, and run gathering threads along raw edges (8). Position rings over knob and draw up to fit. Stitch by hand to hold gathered fullness (9). Drape curtains to side, looping them behind rosettes.

BATHROOM RUFFLES

A small window makes a challenging project but the scale makes it a less daunting task. This window has had the full treatement and the roller blind has been finished off with a strip of broderie anglaise to keep the dainty feel. You will need enough fabric to cover the width of the window 1½ times for both valance and curtains – allow more fabric for ruffles. You will also need a wooden batten and curtain wire or rod for the valance, and heading tape and curtain track for the curtains and braid to finish off. For the roller blind, you need a roller blind kit and fabric, aerosol fabric stiffener and a length of broderie anglaise edging at least 3in (8cm) wide.

Measure up the window (see page 180) and decide on the position for the curtain track. Fix up the track and fix a batten above it to hold the valance. The finished valance should extend beyond the curtains by 1in (2.5cm) on either side.

For the valance, join strips of fabric to make a width 1½ times the length of the valance batten. The depth of the strip should be about ⅓ the height of the window. Draw up a paper pattern the shape of half the finished valance.

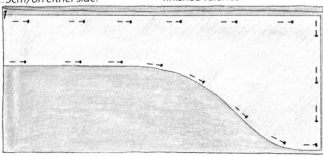

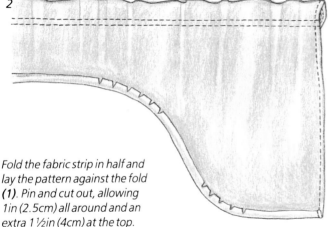

Fold the fabric strip in half and lay the pattern against the fold (1). Pin and cut out, allowing 1in (2.5cm) all around and an extra 1½in (4cm) at the top. Turn under and stitch a ½in (12mm) double hem at both outside edges of valance. Turn up a ½in (12mm) single hem to right side along the lower edge, clip the curved edge so it lies flat. Stitch. Turn under ½in (12mm) and then 1½in (4cm) across the top and make two rows of stitching to form a casing (2). Measure the shaped edge and cut a 4in (10cm) wide strip of fabric 1½ times this

length. Turn under a ½in (12mm) double hem around all edges and stitch. Run two rows of gathering through one long edge and draw up ruffle to fit valance. Pin, baste and stitch onto right side of valance. Distribute fullness evenly. Cover stitching with braid, topstitched in place (3).

Cut out the curtains, 1½ times the drawn-up width of the curtain plus 1in (2.5cm) down each side for hems. Decide on the length and lay the two pieces of fabric for the curtains on a flat surface, right sides facing. Shape the inner corners into smooth curves, trimming away at least 2in (5cm) at the

Pin and stitch a standard heading tape across the top of the curtain to cover the raw edge of the hem (4). Do not sew across cords when you turn in and hem short edges of heading tape. Measure the long curved inner edges and across the bottom edge. Cut a 4in (10cm) strip of fabric to 1½ times this length and make up the ruffle as described for the valance (3). Attach the braid as before.

Measure up for the roller blind. Cut fabric to size. Cut a strip of broderie anglaise to fit across the blind, plus 2in (5cm) allowance, and stiffen with an aerosol fabric stiffener. Check against blind for fit, and turn under a double hem along outer edges. Topstitch lace to blind, placing raw edge of lace 2in

lower edge. Turn under ½in (12mm) double hems down the outer edges. Turn under a ½in (12mm) single hem to right side down the long curved inner edges and across the bottom of the curtain. Turn under 1in (2.5cm) single hem across the top, pin and baste in place.

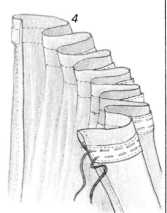

Measure for the tie-backs (see page 41) and cut a strip of fabric 6in (15cm) wide to this length. Fold lengthwise, right sides facing. Stitch down long raw edges to form a tube. Turn right side out and stitch a ring into a 2in (5cm) hem at either end (5).

(5cm) from the bottom edge of the blind. (Hold in place with tape, do not pin or baste.) Turn up 1in (2.5cm) and then 1½in (4cm) to right side of blind, covering the raw edges of the lace. Stitch the casing close to the folded edge (6). Insert batten into casing. Complete blind (see pages 46 and 48).

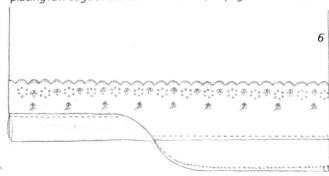

RUFFLED BATHROOM PELMET

If desirable, you can completely alter or disguise the shape of a window. In this case, the window was rather large for a bathroom where privacy and cosiness are preferable. The arched pelmet, cut out of plywood and covered in wallpaper, gives the room a period character and is an unusual focal point at the end of the bath. The fabric is used to make a double ruffle in two colours and is attached around the inner edge of the pelmet. The pelmet is covered in wallpaper but could be covered with fabric. You will need a piece of plywood cut to the size of the window, ¾in (2cm) timber to go around the window recess, wallpaper or fabric for the front and back of the finished pelmet, braid, glue, fabric in two colours for the ruffle and velcro strip.

Cut the ¾in (2cm) timber into strips to fit around the inside of the window recess, with the lower edge of the timber at the level of the bottom of the finished pelmet. In this case, the distance from the top of the window to the skirting board is divided into four to give good proportions (1). The pelmet ends a quarter of the way up the window from the skirting. Fix the timber by screwing it into the window surround every 20in (50cm), positioning it so that the front edge of the timber is set ¼in (6mm) in from the inner edge of the moulding on the window surround. This rebate will allow the pelmet to lie flush with the window frame. Use a large sheet of paper or sheets of lining paper or newspaper taped together to make a pattern for the pelmet. Design your own shape or follow the proportions here (2). The top section is a semi-circle. Using the pattern, mark the pelmet shape onto a piece of plywood that has been cut to fit neatly into the window recess. Cut out the shape with a jigsaw or padsaw. If you do not have a suitable saw, cut the plywood in six separate sections (2). Prepare wallpaper lengths to cover the entire pelmet.

Paper the back (window side) of the pelmet first, bringing the paper round to the front. Slash it and paste neatly down (3). Fix the pelmet to the timber with screws. If you have six pieces, paper each separately and screw them up.

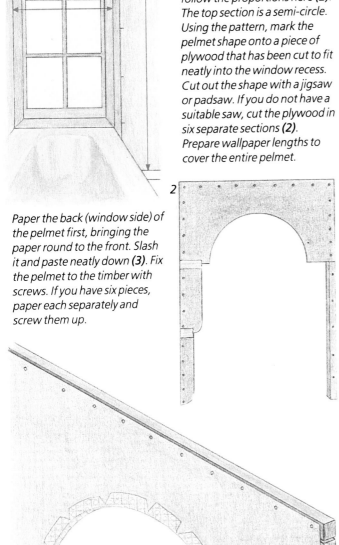

1

2

3

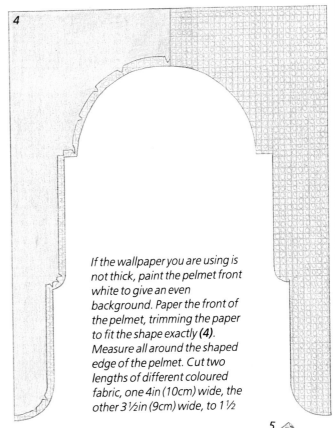

4

If the wallpaper you are using is not thick, paint the pelmet front white to give an even background. Paper the front of the pelmet, trimming the paper to fit the shape exactly (4). Measure all around the shaped edge of the pelmet. Cut two lengths of different coloured fabric, one 4in (10cm) wide, the other 3½in (9cm) wide, to 1½ times the length of the shaped edge. Turn under a ¼in (6mm) double hem along all edges (5). Position the ruffles on top of one another, the wide ruffle underneath with one long edge matching. Run gathering stitches through both layers and pin and stitch the gathers evenly to a tape the finished length of the pelmet shape. Glue lengths of velcro all around the shaped pelmet edge. Stitch the other half to the ruffle (6). Glue braid around the outside edge of the pelmet (7).

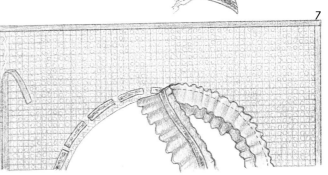

5

6

7

APPLIQUÉD KITCHEN CURTAIN

The appliqué motif on this straight café curtain has been repeated elsewhere in the room to give a it cohesion. You will need fabric for the curtains, off-cuts of red and green for the motifs – these pieces should be about the same weight as the curtain – graph paper for enlarging or reducing the design, dressmaker's carbon paper (or you can trace it directly onto the fabric as described on page 166) and curtain wire or a curtain rod.

Measure your window (see page 180) and cut the fabric to size, adding 1in (2.5cm) on either side and 5½in (14cm) for the top and bottom hems. Turn under ½in (12mm) double hems down either side and pin. Turn up ½in (12mm) and 3in (8cm) across the bottom. Pin and mitre the corners (see page 178). Machine stitch side and bottom hems. Across the top of the curtain, turn under ½in (12mm) and then 1½in (4cm) and stitch to make a casing (1).

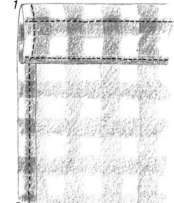

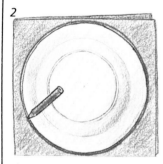

Enlarge the clover leaf design on page 167. Choose a round plate larger than the flower design. Place the plate on the red fabric and draw around it (2). Cut out and repeat for each flower motif. Trace the flower design onto tracing paper (3). Place a piece of dressmaker's carbon paper, right sides facing, onto the red fabric.

Place tracing centrally on the fabric over the carbon. Pin in place and draw over the internal design lines and the outer shape. This transfers the motif to the red fabric. Pin the fabric motifs in position on the right side of curtain (4).

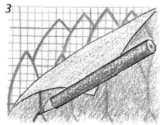

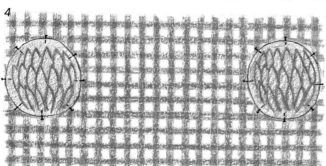

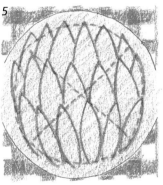

Baste around and through the flower motif to hold in place *(5)*. Stitch around the design with a small zigzag stitch, working each petal in turn following the marked lines on the fabric *(6)*. Pull all threads through to the wrong side and fasten off. (You may need to practise the stitch size on an off-cut to achieve a satin-stitch effect.)

Carefully cut away all excess fabric from around the flower with sharp embroidery scissors *(7)*. Complete the design with the leaves for the flower and the clover leaves *(8)*. Finally, using a wider zigzag stitch on your machine, make the lines for the stalks, having first marked them on the curtain fabric with a soft pencil. Take care not to sew across the flower leaves.

DRAPED CURTAINS

This idea has a lot of style and requires very little sewing. It is purely decorative as the curtains are not designed to draw. You will need a reversible fabric (both sides show) at least 47in (120cm) wide, velcro strip and a decorative pole – though a plastic drainpipe and two plastic balls would give the same impression.

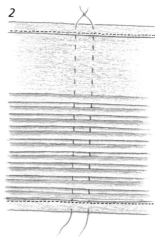

Fix a pair of brackets to the wall to hold the pole in position. Measure up for the fabric (1). Measure from the skirting board, over the pole at one end, down to the window, back over the pole, down to the window again, then back over the pole and down to the skirting board. Allow extra fabric to drape on the floor and 2in (5cm) hem allowance. To make this job easier, drape a piece of string in the position of the finished curtains, and measure that. The fabric you buy must be at least 47in (120cm) wide. The curtain is made from a single width. Turn under a ½in (12mm) single hem along the selvedges. (Make a double hem if the selvedges do not match the fabric.) Mark the two points where the fabric sits over the pole on the outer edges. Run two rows of gathering stitches across the width of the fabric at this point to make large pleats (2).

Cut two lengths of velcro to half the width of the curtain. Draw up the pleating so that the curtain is half its original width. Pin and stitch a strip of velcro to the wrong side of the curtain at the first pleating point on the left of the window, distributing the pleats evenly (3). Repeat for the second row of pleating, stitching the velcro to the right side of the curtain. At the centre point, pleat the fabric width. Cut another strip of velcro to ⅔ the width of the curtain. Draw up the pleats and pin and baste the velcro along on the right side of the curtain. Check drape before stitching. Hem the bottom of curtain.

To wrap the ball finials on the pole, cut a circle of fabric with diameter slightly larger than the ball's circumference. Match the circle centre with the outermost point on the ball. Wrap fabric around ball, pleating in the fullness. Stitch in place by hand. Wrap the pole in fabric. Glue or staple the raw edges along one side and overlap other edge, first turning under a hem to neaten. Stitch neatened short ends to the pleats on the ball. Take strips of velcro and stitch the shorter lengths to the fabric cover on the pole at each end (4). Stitch the longer length to the fabric at the centre back of the pole. Fold fabric in half at the centre point and drape over pole, matching the velcro strip. Loop the curtain over the outer edges so that the drapes are of even length.

WINDOW DRESSING IDEAS

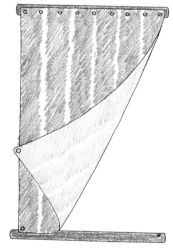

Below *Some windows are comparatively difficult to dress because there is no room for curtains or because they are sloped, as in an attic. This idea can be adapted to any window shape. Cut a piece of fabric to the shape of the window, allowing hem allowance all around. Topstitch the hems and make sail-type holes with an eyelet punch and eyelets or make them like a buttonhole (see page 176). Fix the curtain over hooks screwed into the window surround to correspond with the holes.*

Above *Cleverly designed curtains can create all kinds of optical illusions. Even the simplest idea, like the curtain here, can give the impression of an unusually shaped window. The wooden curtain pole, which is resting on two coat hooks (not shown as the curtains are looped up over them), has been split in two lengthwise and the curtains are gathered and stapled in place along the flat edge. The other half of the pole is screwed back to hide the staples. The drape of the curtain is the most important touch. Swooped back, almost off the floor, the resulting opening looks arched and faintly Gothic, although the window may be an ordinary rectangle.*

Left *To curtain an arched window or doorway, cut a template out of tissue in the shape of the arch. Then extend the pattern lengthways until it matches up to the distance between the highest point of the arch and the bottom of the proposed curtain hem. Lay the pattern out on a flat surface and place the fabric onto it, gather it up into natural-looking folds. Cut out the resultant curved edge and gather up by hand onto a tape to correspond with the line of the arch. Attach rings to the tape holding the curtain, and put them over hooks screwed to the window surround. You will have to make tie-backs (see page 41) to hold the curtains back.*

Left *If you have a beautiful piece of old lace, this is a simple and effective way to show it off. Simply fold the lace in two widthwise and place it over a decorative curtain pole. Scoop each half back and arrange over brass tie-back holders. The success of this idea does depend on finding the right length of lace to fit the window. If you cannot, then buy a length of lace and hem the raw edges or finish them with a deep ruffle.*

Below *You can create a four-poster effect over a bed with two decorative curtain poles attached to the wall just below the ceiling and on the ceiling about 36in (91cm) out from the first pole. Buy a length of light flimsy lace and drape it over the poles. The lace needs to be about 48in (122cm) wide for an average double bed.*

Below *To echo the colours in a room and co-ordinate sheer café curtains, sew bands of coloured ribbon onto the made-up curtains to create a harlequin pattern. Bind the edges with matching ribbon (or satin bias binding) and make tabs of ribbon to slide the curtain rod through.*

3

SITTING PRETTY

Making your own loose covers is one of the biggest jobs in home sewing but not as difficult as is often assumed. It is a tremendous saving in terms of cost, and the effect of just re-covering one armchair in a room can be quite dramatic. Other chairs and sofas can be visually revived with a new collection of pretty cushions, and foam blocks covered in fabric can make a window seat or a sofa simple.

FLOOR CUSHIONS

Simple seating arrangements like this one can be very effective and require no resort to upholstery tools. Here the seating is made up of solid foam blocks and soft floor cushions. The foam blocks can be cut to length to fit any alcove or floor space and the cushions provide a soft alternative. By covering all the cushions in the same fabric, the seating provides a background for other design ideas. You will need a strong, washable, plain-weave fabric for the cushions, foam shapes, cushion pads filled with wadding or kapok and zips for all the covers. The sewing principles in this project form the basis for all box-shaped and regular cushion covers.

If the fabric is not pre-shrunk, wash it first to reduce shrinkage. For the filling, use blocks of firm latex or polyether foam cut to size. So that the cover is easy to remove, the zip fastener is inserted centrally along one short end of the welt, extending around the adjoining corners. Cut the welt piece

equal to the length of the zip plus 1in (2.5cm) and the depth of the foam cushion plus 2in (5cm). Cut the strip in two lengthwise, turn in one long edge of each piece for ½in (12mm) and press. Baste zip in position (1) and machine stitch along both sides.

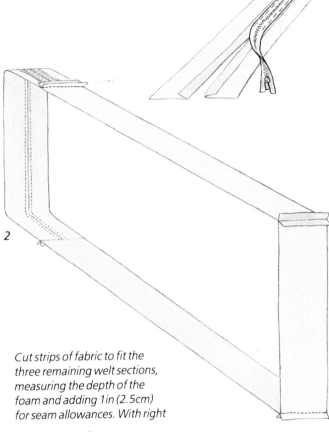

2

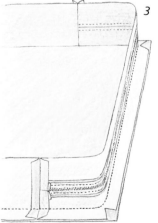

3

Cut strips of fabric to fit the three remaining welt sections, measuring the depth of the foam and adding 1in (2.5cm) for seam allowances. With right sides facing, pin, baste and stitch welt sections together with ½in (12mm) seams. Press seams open (2). Measure top of foam shape and cut two rectangles of fabric plus seam allowances. Pin and baste bottom to one edge of welt with right sides facing (3). (To sew boxed corners see page 178.) Open zip and join to top section in the same way. Press seams towards the welt, turn out and press. Insert foam block.

To make cushion pads for square floor cushions, choose strong, closely woven fabrics, such as cambric. Cut two pieces to the required size with ½in (12mm) seam allowance all around (4). Join pieces together with French seams (see page 177) (5), leaving an opening of 4¾–6in (12–15cm) along the centre of one side.

4

5

Stuff the pad with the filling (see page 182). Reduce mess by pinning or basting the bag containing the filling to the pad and shaking the contents through (6). Push the filling well away from the opening, fold in raw edges, pin and topstitch through all thicknesses close to the edge.

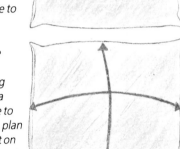

6

To determine the size of the cushion, measure the pad across the centre (7), adding ½in (12mm) all around for a tight fit. If several covers are to be made in the same fabric, plan the most economical layout on graph paper before cutting out.

7

With right sides facing, baste along one edge of the cushion cover. Stitch for 2in (5cm) at either end of seam and press open. Lay zip face down on wrong side with teeth centred along the basted seam. Pin and

stitch (8). Remove basting and open zip. With right sides facing, stitch cushion cover together along other three sides. Trim corners (9), turn out and press. Insert cushion pad.

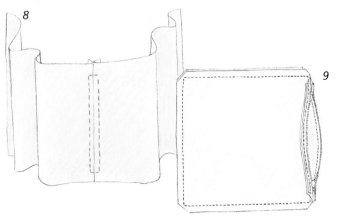

8

9

GINGHAM SEAT COVERS

Here is a timeless remedy for softening the contours of a bentwood chair — a seat cover that you can make in a couple of hours. Depending on what thickness you want for the cushion pad, you need not insert a zip into the cushion. Terylene wadding is machine washable and you could make the seat cover with a piece of ½in (12mm) wadding sewn into the seams; make the pad and cover all in one. However, for extra comfort, you may decide to make them separately.

The visual freshness of this kitchen owes much to the simple use of bright green edging on the scallop-shaped pelmet and the gingham lampshade. The pelmet is hung like a straight, ungathered curtain from a headboard or a curtain track. To make four chair covers you will need 2¼ yards (2 metres) of fabric, the same amount of interfacing and 1 square yard (1 square metre) of thin foam, 3 yards (2.75 metres) of ribbon and four 12in (30cm) long zips.

Make a rough paper pattern of the seat of the chair **(1)**. Fold the pattern into quarters. Make a circle the radius of the seat (see page 106) on your paper pattern, cut out and unfold. Place on the chair to check for size. Using the pattern, cut out two pieces of fabric and two of interfacing, allowing ½in (12mm) seam allowance all around. Cut out one piece of thin foam **(2)**.

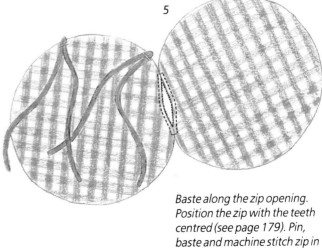

1

5

Baste along the zip opening. Position the zip with the teeth centred (see page 179). Pin, baste and machine stitch zip in place using the zipper foot on your machine **(5)**.

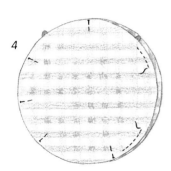

2

Open the zip and with right sides facing stitch around the rest of the cover. Trim and clip the seam allowance **(6)**.

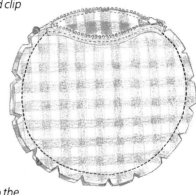

6

Turn the cushion cover to the right side through the zip opening. Press. Trim about ½in (12mm) from all around the foam pad with a sharp knife or long-bladed scissors. Insert the foam into the cover and close the zip **(7)**.

Iron interfacing to wrong side of each fabric piece and cut two lengths of ribbon 12in (30cm) long. Fold in half and pin to right side of fabric so that the ribbons align with the back struts of the chair **(3)**.

3

7

4

Place right sides of the cover together, measure the length of the zip along one side and mark. Stitch for 2in (5cm) at each end of zip opening **(4)**.

FLORAL SEAT COVERS

This is one of the easiest ways to upholster a wooden-frame dining chair. It consists of two covered pads tied to the chair with opulent bows which makes for an unexpectedly pretty back view. The ties have to be positioned to fit the design of the chair frame and if you choose a large, geo-metric or flowery pattern make sure that the most important motif consistently occupies the central position. For each chair you will need the fabric of your choice — a glazed cotton or chintz would be ideal — foam shapes, piping cord and button moulds.

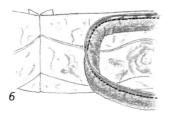

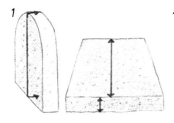

Measure the chair seat and back and make a paper pattern for each cushion. Using the pattern, cut out foam shapes to size *(1)*. For each seat cushion, cut out top and bottom and four welt pieces with ½in (12mm) allowance all around. If using a floral fabric, centre the covers over the pattern *(2)*. Cut four ties 3in (8cm) wide and 36in (93cm) long. Pin two tie pieces together, right sides facing. Measure in from one end 2¼in (6cm) and cut from this point to the end of the tie.

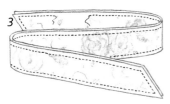

This slants the ends. Stitch all around, leaving an opening on one side *(3)*. Trim and turn to right side. Turn in open edges and slipstitch closed. Fold tie in half and pin fold to short end of one welt piece. Repeat with

other tie. Pin and stitch welts together *(4)* catching the ties in the seams. Begin and end the seams of the welt sections ½in (12mm) in from outer edges. This will make the corners easier to sew.

Make up piping cord (see page 178). Pin and stitch down complete length of piping close to cord *(5)*.

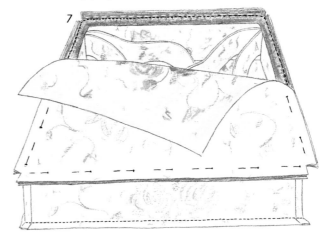

Pin piping all around the welt *(6)*, ½in (12mm) in from the raw edge. Clip into piping at each corner for a good fit. At centre back cut piping so it butts

together. Cut a 1in (2.5cm) strip of matching fabric, trim and turn under both edges and wrap it over the cut ends of piping. Sew across the strip to hold. Baste piping in place. Place one cushion cover to the welt, right sides facing, pin, baste and stitch around all four sides. Match ties to back corners. Spread out seam allowances at corners of welt to get a good shape.

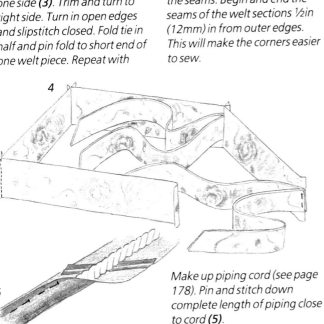

Pin and stitch the other cover in place *(7)*, leaving an opening in the back seam. Trim, turn out and press. Insert foam and slipstitch closed.

Make up ties for back cushion and stitch to right side of back cushion piece *(8)*, matching it

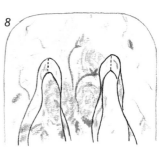

with the struts of your chair. Make up the back cushion with piping (see page 73). Clip into seam allowances on curves for a good fit *(9)*. Insert foam and slipstitch closed.

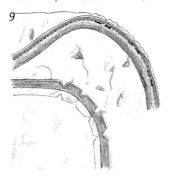

Cover buttons in same fabric and, using a long needle, stitch buttons in place back to back on either side of the cushion *(10)*.

PILLOW SOFA

This two-seater sofa is simply made out of pillows tied to blocks of foam. The white cotton cushion covers are bound in primary colours and the covers slip off easily for washing. You will need medium- and lightweight cotton fabric for the sofa and the pillows, foam shapes cut to measure, eight pillows and the materials to make two smaller cushion pads plus the filling, velcro strip, zips and packets of ½in (12mm) wide bias binding in four primary colours.

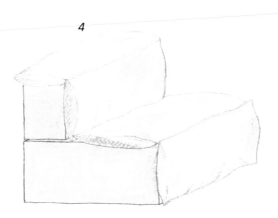

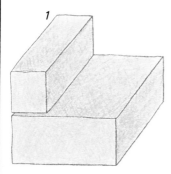

Assemble two chairs from dense foam squabs (1) to make up the finished sofa. If you are using bought pillows, measure these first and have the foam cut so that the pillows will fit along the front, on the seat and against the back of the sofa (4).

To make the ties to attach the pillows to the sofa, using the photograph for reference, cut out the required number in each colour from ½in (12mm) wide bias binding. Each tie should be 12in (30cm) long. Fold each strip lengthwise and topstitch

along outside edge and neaten one short end. Make covers for each of the foam squabs following the method for box cushions (see page 71). Fit zips for easy removal.

Position pillows on chairs to check for fit. Remove excess filling from them if they appear too bulky. (This might be a problem with the pillows that hang down the sofa front.) Measure the head of the sofa and make two cushion pads (see page 71) to these

dimensions. Fill the cushion pads and slipstitch closed. Measure up the finished size of the six large and the two smaller pillows (5). Add ¾in (2cm) to the width and 2½in (6.5cm) to the length. Cut out two rectangles of fabric to the required size for each pillowcase.

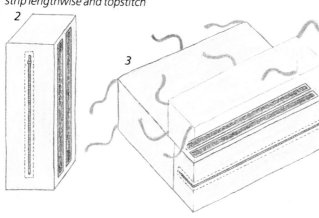

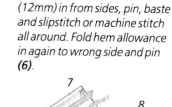

Fit covers over foam shapes (2) and arrange them to form a sofa. Following the photograph again, pin bias ties to the corners and the centres of the shapes where necessary to correspond with the pillow positions (3). Remove covers from foam shapes and either unpick the seam and slip the tie into the seam and stitch, or stitch them in place by hand

with strong double thread. Cut strips of velcro equal to the width of the seat and slipstitch two rows on the underside of the back cover close to the outside edges. Slipstitch the facing velcro strips to the top of the cover to correspond (3). Insert foam shapes again and arrange sofa by joining velcro strips.

Turn in ¼in (6mm) along one short edge of pillowcase bottom to wrong side and press. Turn in and press a further 2in (5cm) and open out last fold. With a strip of velcro close to first fold and ½in

(12mm) in from sides, pin, baste and slipstitch or machine stitch all around. Fold hem allowance in again to wrong side and pin (6).

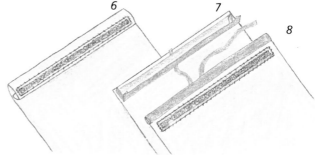

Trim away 2 ¼in (5.5cm) from correspondidng edge of pillow top and centre a 12in (30cm) bias tie on right side of raw edge. Pin and stitch bias binding to the raw edge of pillowcase, catching in the tie, and turning in the raw ends for ¼in (6mm) *(7)*. Fold binding to wrong side and hem neatly. Attach corresponding velcro strip just below hem to match opposite edge *(8)*. With wrong sides facing and velcro strips joined, pin and baste around remaining edges.

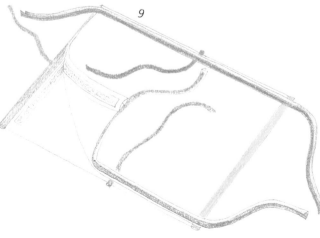

9

Pin bias ties to centre of long edges, then pin and stitch lengths of binding over them, extending 12in (30cm) beyond either end *(9)*. Finish off as before, topstitching extending ties. Make seven more covers in the same way, using the photograph above for colour reference and positions of ties. Insert pillows into their covers and tie pillow to pillow and pillow to sofa at places where ties correspond.

STRIPED DIVAN

An easy way to create extra seating in a room is to cover low-level cupboards or benches with soft, opulent cushions. You will need the main fabric, piping cord and bias strips in a contrasting colour, a zip, and a cushion pad filled with feathers or wadding chips. If the cushions along the back prove to be too floppy, secure them in an upright position by fixing them to a wooden batten on the wall. You will also need velcro and glue or staples.

Cut two pieces of fabric measuring the length by the width of the box-shaped feather cushion pad, plus 1in (2.5cm) all around. Cut a strip of fabric the depth of the pad plus 1in (2.5cm) and the length of the pad all around plus 1in (2.5cm) allowance (1). If you are using striped fabric, cut the welt piece so that the stripes on the long welt contrast with the cushion top. Where a number of cushions are to be made from the same fabric, plan the most economical lay-out on graph paper before cutting out.

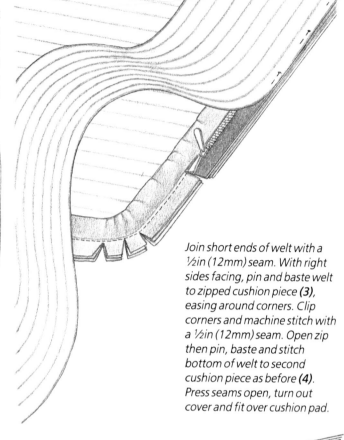

Cut a length of piping cord to fit all around the cushion, cover with a 1½in (4cm) wide bias strip and baste. With right sides facing and starting in the centre of one side, baste piping to cushion along seam line. Snip into seam allowance of piping and join ends neatly. Stitch all around. Pipe second cushion piece in the same way. Open zip and place face down on one side of cushion 2in (5cm) in from either end and with teeth close to stitching line of piping. Pin, baste and machine stitch along centre of zip tape. Close zip, clip fabric through to seam allowance at either end and press seam inwards (2).

Join short ends of welt with a ½in (12mm) seam. With right sides facing, pin and baste welt to zipped cushion piece (3), easing around corners. Clip corners and machine stitch with a ½in (12mm) seam. Open zip then pin, baste and stitch bottom of welt to second cushion piece as before (4). Press seams open, turn out cover and fit over cushion pad.

To prevent back cushions sliding down, anchor them to a narrow wooden batten screwed onto the wall behind. Position batten at a height where it will be concealed by cushions and fix a strip of velcro along its length with strong adhesive or staples. Cut facing velcro strip into three equal pieces and slipstitch to reverse side of cushions to correspond with position of batten. Press velcro strips together.

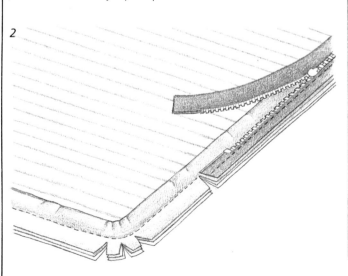

PLAY CUSHIONS

Given the imagination of a child, an ordinary cardboard box can be a ship one moment, a house or spaceship the next. This segmented cushion offers similar opportunities and endless scope for games. Set on end to form a circle, it becomes a fortress under attack. Rolled up at one end to make a pillow, it turns into a raft or a comfortable seat.

The design is made up of seven segments, not unlike a quilt or duvet, but with one castellated edge, and each segment is filled with foam chips or washable terylene wadding. It is made out of traditional mattress ticking, which is tough and not expensive, but any striped material will do. (The stripes are an advantage when there are long straight lines to be stitched.) You will need 5½ yards (5 metres) of 36in (91cm) wide fabric (check that the fabric is pre-shrunk, if not you should wash it before you cut it out), the filling material, five 1in (2.5cm) buttons, five smaller buttons and strong tape for the button loops.

From the striped fabric, cut out and make up two pieces each to a finished length of 88 × 33in (225 × 84cm). Stitch any fabric lengths together with straight seams and press open. Place both pieces with right sides facing, matching the edges and aligning stripes if possible. Follow the diagram opposite *(1)* and cut one long edge into turret shapes; 12in (30cm) across for each section and 6in (15cm) deep. Pin and stitch along the top edge and down one side, taking a ½in (12mm) seam allowance. Cut across the corners and trim the seam allowance.

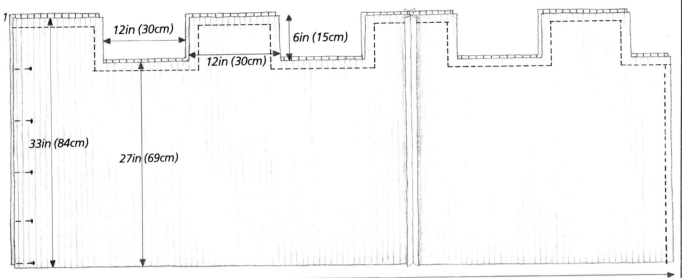

1

12in (30cm)

6in (15cm)

12in (30cm)

33in (84cm)

27in (69cm)

88in (225cm)

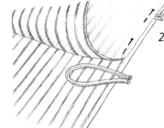

2

Cut five 3in (8cm) lengths of cord for button loops. Position them down the short open edge (2) at about 6in (15cm) intervals, beginning with a loop at the bottom edge. Pin and stitch the seam, catching the loops.

3

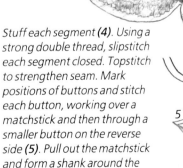

Trim the seam and turn to the right side. Press and turn in raw edges along open edge and baste hems in place. Divide the entire piece into equal vertical segments, about 5½in (14cm) apart, and mark. Pin and topstitch along each marked line through all layers (3).

4

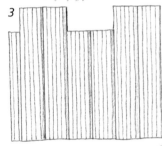

Stuff each segment (4). Using a strong double thread, slipstitch each segment closed. Topstitch to strengthen seam. Mark positions of buttons and stitch each button, working over a matchstick and then through a smaller button on the reverse side (5). Pull out the matchstick and form a shank around the thread.

5

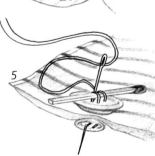

Those cushion covers are made by the simplest possible method. You will need a foam shape cut to size and about 3-4in (8-10cm) thick, fabric, lining fabric, a zip equal in length to the width of the foam less 4in (10cm), and for the pleated cushion about ½ yard (45cm) each of the fabric and a contrasting fabric for the pleated edging.

Measure the length and width of the seat and cut a piece of foam at least 3-4in (8-10cm) thick, a fraction smaller all around than the area it is to fill. Measure length and width of foam and add depth of one side *(1)* plus ½in (12mm) seam allowance on all sides. Cut out two pieces of fabric to these dimensions. With right sides facing, pin and baste together

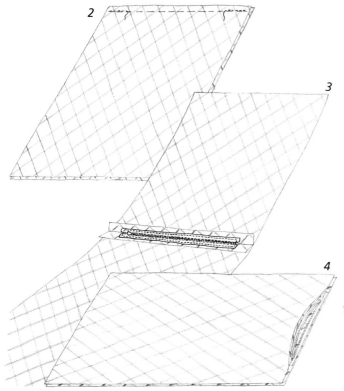

at one short edge, machine stitch for 2in (5cm) at either end of basted seam *(2)* and insert zip (see page 71) *(3)*. Remove basting thread and open zip. With right sides facing *(4)*, pin and stitch remaining sides and press seams open.

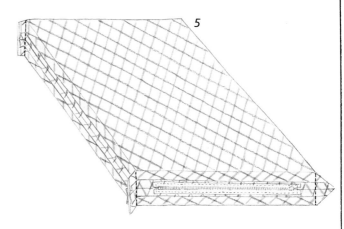

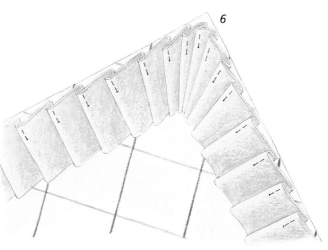

With bag inside out, place over foam squab, centring seams along sides and pin and baste seam allowance at corners. Remove cover and machine stitch seams across corners. Cut away excess fabric. Press seam inward *(5)*. Turn cover to right side through zip opening and ensure perfect corners by pushing a blunt scissor blade up inside the points. Make a lightweight lining for the foam in the same way, omitting the zip and topstitching the opening closed. Insert foam into cushion cover and close zip. By lining the foam shape you give the window seat a longer life as the foam breaks down in time.

Measure the cushion pad (see page 71) and cut out two pieces of fabric for the cushion cover. For the pleated edging, cut a strip of fabric equal to twice the length around the cushion and at least 4in (10cm) wide. Fold strip lengthwise with right sides out. Starting at the centre point of one side, pin edge of fabric strip to one cushion piece with raw edges matching. Make the first pleat 2in (5cm) along from the outer edge. Fold strip over for ½in (12mm) and pin at the top through all layers. Start next pleat about 1in (2.5cm) along from the centre of the first and pin. Continue in this way, leaving less fabric between pleats at corners to allow for the extra fullness required *(6)*. Join raw edges of ruffle and baste all pleats around cushion cover. Make up cushion (see pages 71 and 98).

LOOSE COVERS

Making your own loose covers is undoubtedly a great saving and the revitalizing effect on a room is quite dramatic. Take time to consider the different possibilities of contrasting piping and the style of skirt you want. Make a cutting plan to help you to work out the amount of fabric needed. Fabrics should be hardwearing with a firm weave but not too heavy, as the layers of fabric and piping will make sewing difficult. You will need enough extra fabric for the bias strip, (if you use a contrast fabric, it needs to be hard wearing or the piping will fray and your work will be spoiled), heavyweight piping cord, cord or tape for the bottom casing and press-stud tape for the fastening.

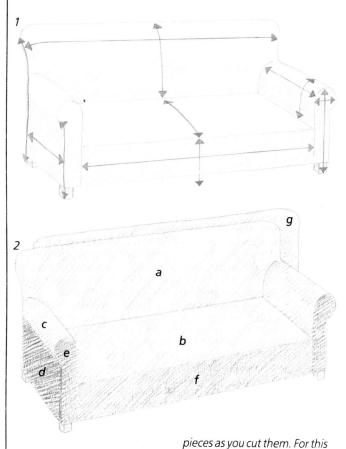

Following the existing cover, decide on the positions of the seam lines and measure up for each section. Take the measurements for each section at the widest point (1). Measure to the floor and allow for the tuck-in around the seat. Make notes and use a system of letters to refer to the pieces as we have done here (2). Mark the letter in tailor's chalk on the fabric pieces as you cut them. For this style of sofa you will need:

a inside back – add 6in (15cm) along lower edge where back meets seat and arms.
b seat – add tuck-in around sides and back.
c inside arm – cut 2; add tuck-in along back and lower edges.
d outside arm – cut 2.
e front arm (scroll) – cut 2.
f front seat.
g outside back.

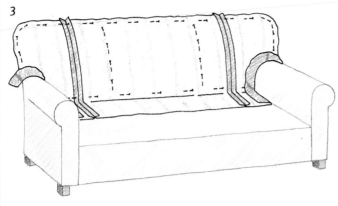

3

Baste along pinned seams at back of arm and around tuck-in allowance. Clip into curves. Turn cover right side out and check for fit. Remove and stitch the basted seams. Trim allowances and neaten raw edges with zigzag stitching or pinking shears. Replace cover on sofa, inside out, and pin sections in place to keep them taut while you work (6).

Now join the outside arm (d). The seam along the arm may be piped but pin without piping at this stage. Piping can be added

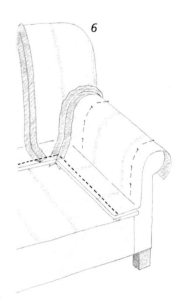

6

Make a cutting plan on graph paper and calculate amount of fabric required. Cut out a rectangle for each section allowing 1in (2.5cm) all around. Join fabric to make up widths for inside back (a). Press seams open. Lay inside back right side down onto back of sofa. Pin to sofa around edges (3). Lay seat section (b) onto seat and pin to sofa (4). Fold up tuck-in allowance from inside back and seat.

7

when you replace the pins with basting stitches. Pin outer arm to sofa and pin seam line (7).

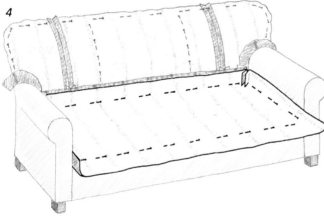

4

The diagram (8) indicates where the piping should run. Measure the total length of piping required and make up, using 4in (10cm) wide bias cut strips folded around heavyweight piping cord (see page 178). Piping may match or contrast with cover fabric. Remove cover, baste seam, inserting the piping as you work. Turn right side out and check for fit. Remove and stitch the seam, trim seam allowance and neaten raw edge.

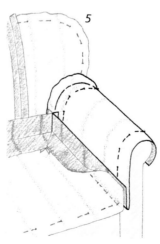

5

Trim fabric roughly to fit shape of sofa. Lay inside arm section (c) over sofa arm and pin in place (5). Trim away excess where necessary, not to less than 1in (2.5cm) and do not trim tuck-in allowance. Pin the unpiped seams around the seat and the back of the arm. Pin the edges of the tuck-in allowance together, right sides facing. Check that you will be able to tuck the allowance in. Remove the cover from the sofa.

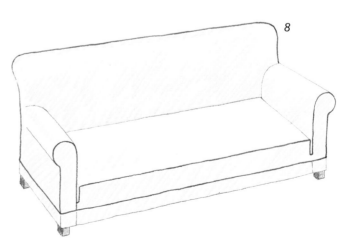

8

9

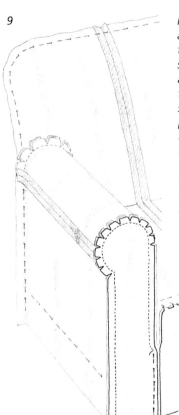

Replace cover and pin to sofa around unstitched edges. Tuck tuck-in allowance down around sides and back of seat. Pin front arm section (*e*) to sofa and pin to inner and outer arms along seam line. Baste and insert piping. Stitch around front arm up to tuck-in section of seat (*9*). Clip curves.

Pin front seat section (*f*) to sofa and pin along seam line to seat section, tuck-in allowance and front arm (*10*). Remove, baste, insert piping, and check for fit before stitching. Trim and neaten as before.

10

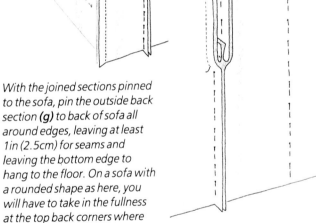

13

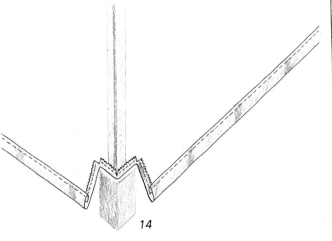

With the joined sections pinned to the sofa, pin the outside back section (*g*) to back of sofa all around edges, leaving at least 1in (2.5cm) for seams and leaving the bottom edge to hang to the floor. On a sofa with a rounded shape as here, you will have to take in the fullness at the top back corners where the inside back meets the outside back. Either run a row of gathering stitches around the top shaped corner (*11*) of the inside back and draw up the fullness to fit the outside back, or take in the fullness by pinning

narrow pleats (*12*). Topstitch the pleats in place. Pleats should be even and all running in the same direction.

Pin outside back to inside back all around the top edge. At one end, pin sides together down to the floor level. Leave the other side open below the level of the arm to fit fastening tape (*13*). Remove cover and baste, inserting piping as you work. Check for fit and stitch. Trim and neaten as before.

Trim away fabric around legs at corners. Turn under a ½in (12mm) hem around legs and stitch. Trim raw edges with pinking shears. Turn up ¼in (6mm), then 1in (2.5cm) all around lower edge. Pin, baste and stitch to form a casing (*14*). Turn cover right side out and fit on sofa. Pin opening closed down side.

11

12

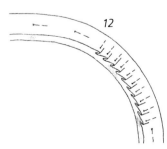

14

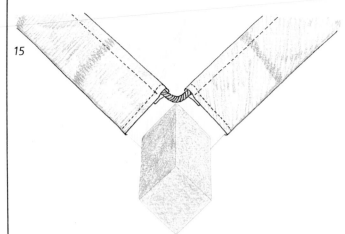

15

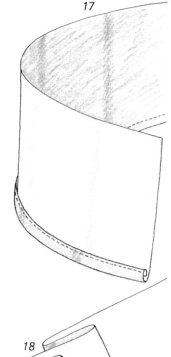

17

Turn up a double ½in (12mm) hem all around lower edge of skirt. Pin, baste and stitch **(17)**.

To form the pleats, pin the skirt section to the sofa along the marked line. Start at opening. Leave ¾in (2cm) hem allowance. Make the first fold 4in (10cm) from the corner. Turn 4in (10cm), then turn back 8in (20cm), then fold back 4in (10cm). Continue pinning the skirt to the next corner. Make the first fold 4in (10cm) from the corner and repeat the folding pattern, reversing it on the other side of the corner **(18)**. Repeat until all pleats are pinned. Press pleats, and stitch across the top to hold **(19)**. Hem ends of skirt so that the hems line up with the raw edges of the seam allowance at the opening.

Measure the length of the casing and cut a length of cord plus 12in (30cm). Thread the cord through the casing beginning at the opened side. Draw up the cover tightly under the sofa, threading the cord behind the legs at corners so that ends of casing are drawn

together **(15)**. Trim and neaten fabric at opening corner. If you are not adding a skirt, the opening fastenings can be fitted at this stage **(22)**. If you are adding a skirt, decide on the finish. You can add a frilled skirt or, as here, a straight skirt with pleats at each corner.

16

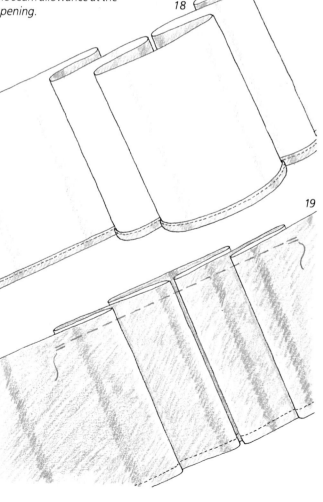

18

19

Mark a chalk line horizontally around the sofa where the top of the skirt is to be attached **(16)**. Ensure that the line is exactly the same distance from the floor all around the sofa. Measure the depth of the skirt and add 2in (5cm) allowance. Measure the total length of the skirt adding 32in (80cm) for each of the four double pleats.

Add 1½in (4cm) for seam allowance at ends. Join strips to make up this length. As far as possible, position seams so that they fall in the pleated corner sections or they line up with seams on the outside back section or the front seat. Whatever type of skirt you choose, the depth will be the same but the length will vary.

20

Put in a row of pins down the back opening to mark the finished seam line. Here the fastening is a special press stud tape, but it could equally well be closed with hooks and eyes or a heavy-duty velcro. Turn under a ¼in (6mm) single hem down both raw edges of seam allowance on either side of opening. Zigzag stitch in place. Stitch one half of fastening tape to outside arm section, running onto the skirt which has already been hemmed along its edge. Press the seam allowance of the outside back, back on itself and press the hemmed skirt edge back with it. Pin and stitch the corresponding half of the tape

through all layers, the seam allowance and the outside back and the skirt *(22)*. Stitch down both sides of tape. When the cover is put back on the sofa, the seam allowance of outer arm section should tuck around the back of the sofa and the back section attaches to it there. Take care not to catch in part of the pleat or the casing.

To make the boxed cushions for the sofa, measure the cushion pads. You will need a top, a bottom and a welt to fit right around with piping along both seams where the cover joins the welt. Cut out pieces (see page 78) and pin and baste piping in place on top and bottom sections. Make up as shown on page 78.

22

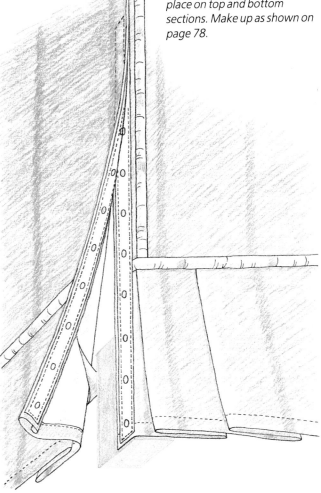

21

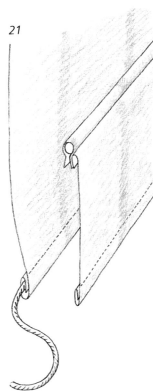

Pin and stitch piping to top edges of skirt on right side so that raw edges of piping match raw edges of skirt. With right sides facing, and with skirt upside down *(20)* pin along stitching line of piping to the marked line on the sofa cover. Remove cover from sofa and baste and stitch skirt in place, enclosing piping in seam. When skirt is stitched, neaten the raw edges of the seam allowance and press the skirt down so that piping stands up at marked chalk line *(21)*. At each end of skirt, trim cord from inside the piping so that it does not add unnecessary bulk to the back opening.

This sofa has been given a softer, less tailored look with a gathered skirt. This finish is best with lighter furnishing fabrics, cottons and linen mixes rather than fabrics with a heavy weave or pile. An unusual touch, which echoes the softness of the skirt, *is the use of a ruched welt around the boxed cushions. To make construction and stitching the gathered seams easier, the zip has been set into the bottom of the cushion cover. Make the loose cover as on pages 84-88.*

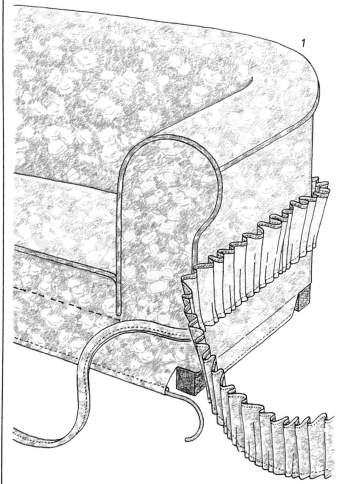

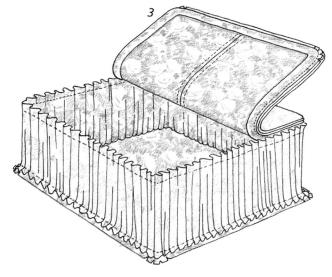

To make up cushions with ruched welts, cut top section ½in (12mm) larger all around than cushion pad. Cut two pieces for the bottom section, each half the size of the cushion pad with ½in (12mm) all around. With right sides facing, baste the two bottom sections together along one length. Stitch over this seam for 2in (5cm) at either end and press seam open. Set zip over seam, centring teeth over basting stitches. Pin and stitch zip in place. Unpick basting. Pin piping around top and bottom sections (2). Baste in place, clipping into seam allowance at corners.

Cut and join strips 1in (2.5cm) wider than depth of cushion and of sufficient length to make a welt 1½ times the length around the cushion pad. Join ends of strips with flat seams to make a loop of fabric. Run rows of gathering stitches along both edges of welt and draw up to fit around cushion. With right sides facing, pin welt to top section of cushion. Baste and stitch around edges along stitching line where piping is joined to cushion cover. Pin bottom section in place (3), open zip and stitch. Neaten seam allowances with a zigzag stitch. Turn right side out and press. Insert cushion pad.

Mark or pin a line around the cover where the top of the skirt is to be stitched. Measure the length around the sofa at this point and join sufficient strips of fabric to make a skirt 1½ times this length. The width should be the depth of the skirt plus 2in (5cm) allowances. Hem the bottom and the short ends and gather up to fit around the sofa. Pin and baste piping to skirt (see *page 89). Distribute fullness evenly. With cover on sofa, pin skirt in place (1), right sides facing, skirt upside down and piping seam line matching the pinned or chalked line on the sofa. Remove cover, baste and stitch skirt to cover. Neaten raw edges and press skirt downwards. Finish opening with a fastening tape as described on page 89.*

QUILTED CUSHIONS

It is the careful finishing touches, like an exquisite cushion, that make a room look complete. The attraction of these quilted designs is that they do not require great artistic skill, just the ability to machine stitch in a straight line. Use a light-weight, delicate material such as silk and back it with special nylon quilted wadding which has diagonal lines stitched on it. Once you have copied these, there are a wealth of other geometric shapes you can explore on your own. There is no reason why the thread should match the colour of the fabric; you could introduce a contrast to echo the other colours in the room.

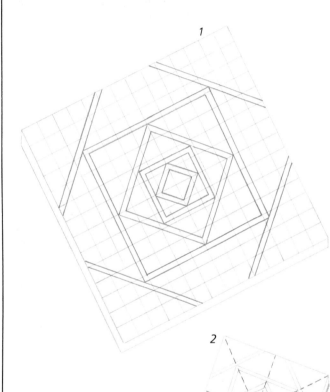

For each cushion cover, cut out two pieces of fabric and one piece of nylon quilting to the required size. Use the stitched quilting lines on the nylon fabric as grid lines and this will make the transposing of the quilting lines much easier. To make the quilting lines, follow the grid lines on the patterns on pages 168-169 and rule them in using a soft pencil (1). If you cannot find nylon quilting fabric, then transpose your quilting lines onto a piece of muslin and baste the muslin to a layer of wadding. Pin and baste around the edges of the cushion cover and through the middle to hold the wadding firmly in place while you quilt the lines (2). You are going to work from the back of this cushion cover.

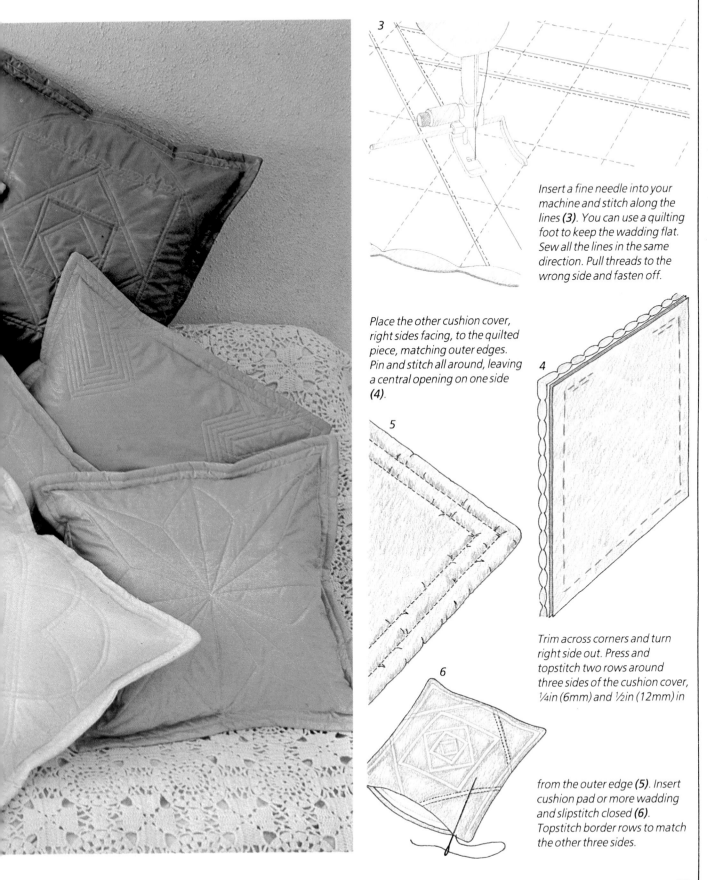

Insert a fine needle into your machine and stitch along the lines (3). You can use a quilting foot to keep the wadding flat. Sew all the lines in the same direction. Pull threads to the wrong side and fasten off.

Place the other cushion cover, right sides facing, to the quilted piece, matching outer edges. Pin and stitch all around, leaving a central opening on one side (4).

Trim across corners and turn right side out. Press and topstitch two rows around three sides of the cushion cover, ¼in (6mm) and ½in (12mm) in from the outer edge (5). Insert cushion pad or more wadding and slipstitch closed (6). Topstitch border rows to match the other three sides.

This selection of cushion ideas involves using a mixture of plain colours and patterns. For an 18in (46cm) square cushion, you will need 1 yard (1 metre) each of the plain and floral fabrics, piping cord and a zip if used. These cushions are ideal for using up off-cuts of fabric. The gathered cushion only takes ¾ yard (70cm) of fabric and contrasting piping.

To make triangles for the envelope cushion, measure cushion pad and cut out two pieces of fabric to size. With right sides facing, pin and stitch two diagonal lines ¼in (6mm) apart across fabric from corner to corner (1). Cut between seam lines and turn out. Press the four triangles. Cut out two pieces for the cushion cover. Position the triangles on the right side of one piece with points meeting in the centre and raw edges matching. Pin and baste (2). Make up piping (see page 178) and pin and stitch piping over triangles (3). Overlap ends of piping and turn down so that raw edges are caught in the seam.

1

2

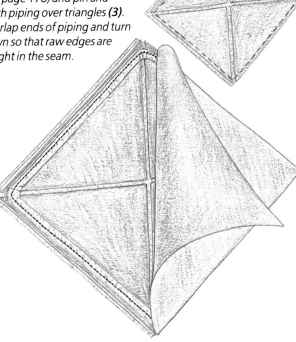

3

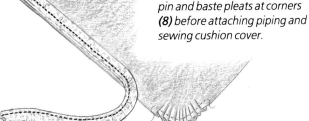

4

Make up rest of cushion (see pages 70, 93 and 98) and attach fabric ties to inner corners of triangles (4).

Cut out four cushion pieces, two from each fabric. Mark the finished size of the inside panel on the right side of one plain piece. Mark another line ½in (12mm) inside the marked panel. Cut out the panel following the inner line and clip into corners. Cut out inner panel from floral fabric, allowing ½in (12mm) all around. Pin into frame, right sides facing (5). Repeat to make the other cushion piece. Face panelled pieces with a floral fabric, right sides together (6). Turn out and slipstitch closed. With framed panels uppermost, pin cushion covers together around the frame seam line. Topstitch together around three

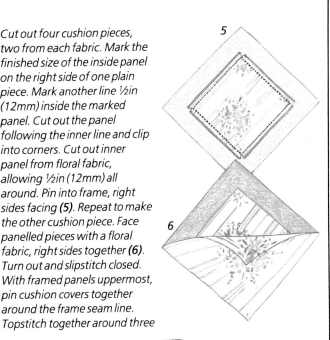

5

6

7

8

sides. (7). Insert cushion pad, topstitch along fourth side of frame and stitch cord over seam.

To gather corners of cushions, pin and baste pleats at corners (8) before attaching piping and sewing cushion cover.

LACE HEARTS

These heart-shaped cushions are ideal for small bits of old lace. For example, lace tablecloths damaged by tea stains and wear may still retain some useful lace motifs. Wash them carefully in special washing powder and cut out the good pieces. For the cushion cover, you need a soft but reliable fabric such as polyester or finely woven silk, and lace strips for the ruffles. If you fill the cushions with washable terylene wadding, they can be cleaned as they are. Alternatively, you can fill them with sweet-smelling pot-pourri. You will also need square and round cushion pads (see page 71), ribbons and press-stud tape or zips.

Cut the heart-shape pattern from paper measuring not less than 14 × 16in (36 × 41cm). Fold the paper in half lengthwise and rule a diagonal line from corner to corner. Place a 7in (17.5cm) plate against the fold and draw around it (1). Cut out around the curve and down the ruled line. To alter the size of the paper pattern, use a longer piece of paper, and scale it up or down by adding or subtracting along the cut edges, tapering off at the top to maintain the heart shape. Cut out two pieces of fabric for the cover.

Centre the lace motif, right side uppermost, on the right side of one piece of the cushion cover. Pin, baste and slipstitch loosely along the outside edges and through the centre with neat running stitches, following the lace design. Make the ribbon into a bow and stitch in place

through both layers (2). Measure around the shape and cut a lace ruffle 1½ times the measurement. Join the raw edges by overlapping them ½in (12mm). Pin and slipstitch loosely together. Gather the lace ruffle by hand along one edge.

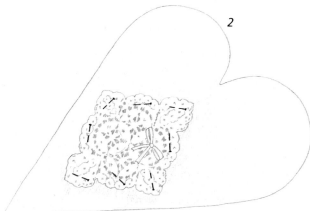

With right sides facing and raw edges together, pin the lace ruffle to the cushion, easing the fullness into the angles and around the curves (3). Join open ends and baste in place.

With right sides facing, pin, baste and machine stitch the cushion covers together, leaving an opening at one side (4). Trim seams and clip curves. Hem both sides of the opening, lay press stud tape over the raw edges and slipstitch along both sides (5).

Make a separate pad (see page 71), fill and insert into the cover. For the smaller wall-hanging cushions, make a hanging loop from ribbon and sew it into the cover with the ruffle (3). The small cushions can be washed in one piece, so omit the press studs, insert a washable terylene wadding and slipstitch closed.

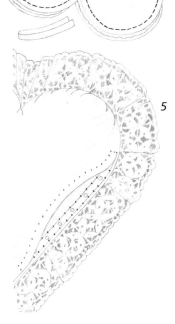

APPLIQUÉD CUSHIONS

One or two star cushions can lift a group. Apart from the random pattern of appliqué and the topstitched strips, all the cushions here are straightforward in their design and yet the overall effect is one of rich variety. You will need fabrics in different but compatible colours for the cushions and the ruffles, appliqué shapes and strips, zips, cushion pads and piping cord.

Cut out cushion cover top and a bottom 1in (2.5cm) wider. Trace the appliqué designs onto the fabric pieces (see motifs on page 170) and cut out shapes. Iron interfacing to wrong side of motifs; any excess can be cut off after stitching. Position the pieces of appliqué on the right side of the cushion top. Begin with the bottom of the design and work upwards. Pin and baste each piece and, using a medium-size zigzag, stitch around the outer edge of each piece, covering the basting stitches (1).

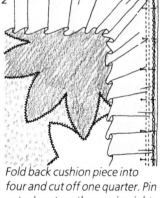

Measure around the outer edge of the cushion top. Make up a 6in (15cm) wide bias strip to twice this length. Stitch the short ends of the strip together, right sides facing, to make a ring. Fold ruffle lengthwise and sew two rows of gathering stitches along the raw edges. Pull up gathers evenly to fit around the edge of the cushion cover. Pin and stitch in place (2).

Fold back cushion piece into four and cut off one quarter. Pin cut edges together again, right sides facing, and stitch 2in (5cm) in from each end, leaving a central opening for the zip (3). Turn back open edges and pin

and stitch zip in place. Open zip. Place two cushion pieces together, right sides facing and ruffle lying towards the centre, pin and stitch around all four sides (4). Trim and turn to right side. Insert cushion pad and close zip.

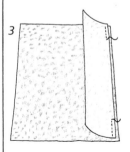

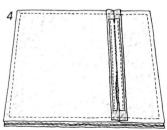

Decide on the dimensions for your framed cushion and cut out four 5in (13cm) wide strips, each one the length of the outside edge (5).

Place short ends of two strips together, right sides facing, and mark the centre point at the short end and points 3in (8cm) down on either side. Sew between these points to intersect at the short raw edge (6). Fasten threads and cut off corners.

Make mitres at the other three corners and turn out the completed frame (7). Topstitch around all sides of frame, close to the outside edge (8). Measure around the inside of the frame and cut out two cushion cover pieces to this size plus ½in (12mm) all around.

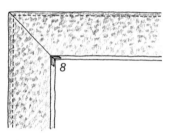

Pin around the central cushion piece, raw edges matching, and clip at the corners (9). Overlap raw edges and hem and neaten exposed bias binding. Make up cushion as for the appliqué cushion (3,4) but keep the zip closed and sew two covers together with wrong sides facing. Stitch all around with a ½in (12mm) seam allowance. Position one edge of mitred border to one side of cushion (10), right sides facing and matching seams to corner points. Pin and stitch together all around. Turn in ½in (12mm) hem allowance on opposite side of border and slipstitch over previous stitching line. Open zip and insert pad.

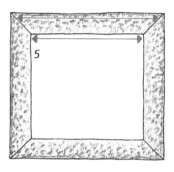

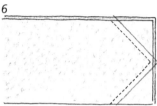

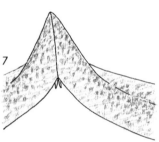

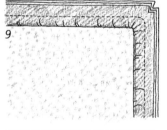

Measure around the panel and make up a length of fabric bias strip to this length plus ½in (12mm) and ¾in (2cm) wide. Fold lengthwise, wrong sides facing, and press.

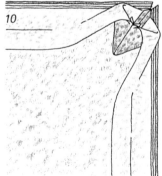

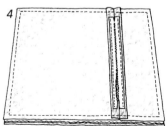

From fabric cut out two cover pieces to the required size. Measure across the cushion cover top to determine the approximate length of each strip. From contrasting fabric cut out 2 ¼in (6cm) wide fabric strips on the straight of grain.

Fold each strip lengthwise with wrong sides facing, press and pin across the cushion piece. Zigzag stitch over raw edges across the whole cover. Pin and stitch five more strips parallel with the first and 1 ¼in (3cm) apart (11). Press strips over the

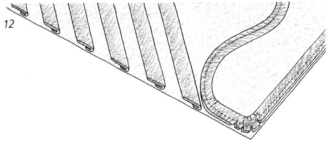

zigzagged edges and pin edges at cushion cover sides. Trim excess fabric away level with cushion sides. Measure around the cushion cover and make up a length of piping in a contrast fabric to this measurement plus ½in (12mm).
Pin and stitch piping around the cushion cover over the

appliquéd strips (12). Join ends together at the centre of one side. Insert zip, either along the piped edge (see page 78) or in the centre back (3,4). Stitch top and bottom cushion cover pieces together. Turn out through zip and insert cushion pad.

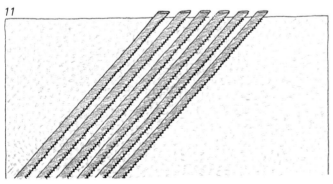

CHAIR AND CUSHION IDEAS

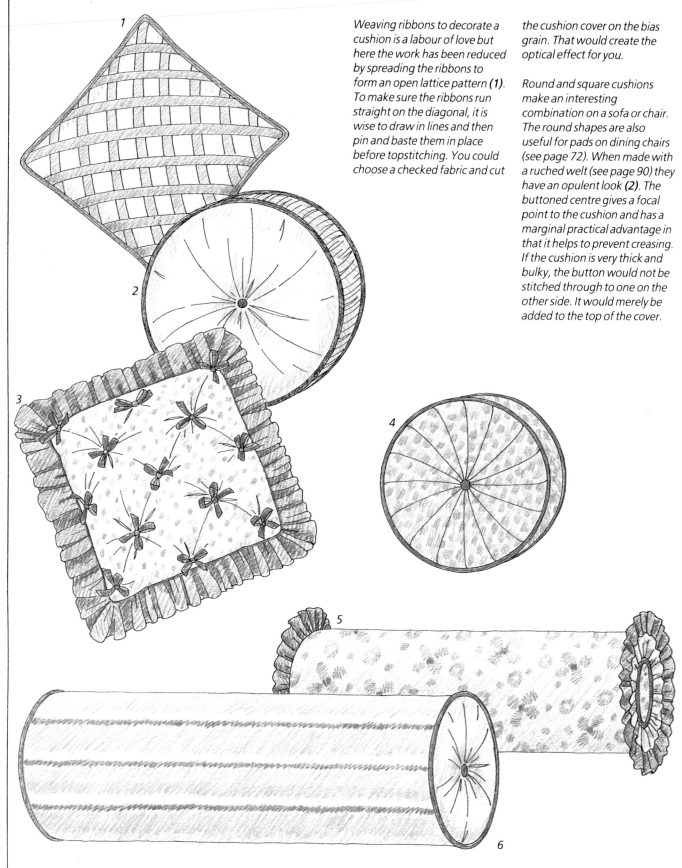

Weaving ribbons to decorate a cushion is a labour of love but here the work has been reduced by spreading the ribbons to form an open lattice pattern *(1)*. To make sure the ribbons run straight on the diagonal, it is wise to draw in lines and then pin and baste them in place before topstitching. You could choose a checked fabric and cut the cushion cover on the bias grain. That would create the optical effect for you.

Round and square cushions make an interesting combination on a sofa or chair. The round shapes are also useful for pads on dining chairs (see page 72). When made with a ruched welt (see page 90) they have an opulent look *(2)*. The buttoned centre gives a focal point to the cushion and has a marginal practical advantage in that it helps to prevent creasing. If the cushion is very thick and bulky, the button would not be stitched through to one on the other side. It would merely be added to the top of the cover.

Bolster-shaped cushions make good back rests. The two variations here include one with a deep double ruffle sewn into the seam which joins the circular end to the bolster (5). To make a bolster cushion, sew a long tube of fabric. The zip is inserted down the side of the tube. The circular ends are then sewn in place (see page 134). The buttoned bolster (6) is made as described above and right (4,8) and the button is covered with fabric to match the piping.

To make a cover for a wicker chair it is best to first make a paper pattern. Cut out the shapes for the cover and sandwich wadding between the cover and the backing. Pipe the edges or bind them to finish off (7). If the design of the wicker work permits, tuck the cover behind the plaited edging to the chair or insert ties and tie the cover at strategic points around the chair. Buttoning the cover helps to keep the wadding firm.

To make this opulent foot stool (8), follow the method (4) but cut out the welt and top and bottom sections to twice the measured length of the welt. The cushion top and bottom strip will only be half the radius. Gather the welt onto piping and then gather the two strips onto the welt. Join side seam. Gather up the long edges and sew onto the cushion pad. Make up a circular tube of fabric to the radius of the central section. Sew the short ends together to make a tube and gather up both edges. Sew the button in place and mount the whole central circle on sturdy interfacing. Turn under the outer edges and hand stitch, inserting piping as you go, to the outer gathered circle.

Make the skirt and cover of this solid foam foot stool (9) like a box-pleated valance (see page 122). The box cushion is piped and filled with soft feathers or kapok (see page 78).

Very feminine and simple to make is the ruffled cushion (3), buttoned with tiny bows.

The pleated circular cushion is piped and buttoned (4). Measure the length and width of the welt. Measure the radius of the pad. Cut out one strip of fabric for the welt and two strips of fabric for the cushion top and bottom. They should be the width of the cushion radius and 1¼ times the length of the welt. Pipe the long edges of the welt strip. Pleat the other two strips onto the welt top and bottom. Join the side seam. You then have a tube of fabric with two rows of piping running through the middle section. Pleat up the two outer edges and run a basting thread through the pleats. Insert the cushion pad and draw up the pleats on the top and bottom of the cushion. Secure and sew a button over the raw edges, threading through to a button on the other side.

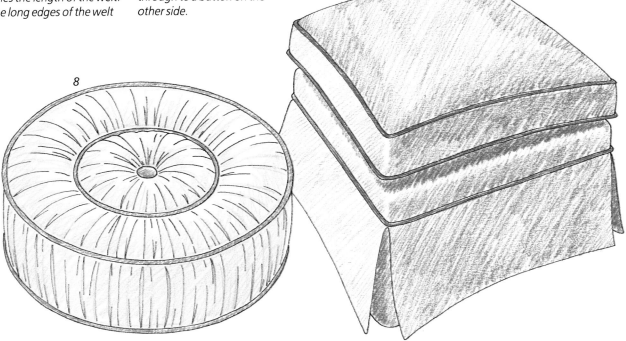

4

TABLE TALK

Apart from protecting your table, a beautifully styled tablecloth can totally transform a dining-room, injecting new life and colour which can easily be altered day by day. A large, round plywood top secured to a small square-top table, and a pretty round tablecloth can mean the difference between seating six and ten. Bedside tables and sofa tables can also look charming covered with floor-length cloths with a shorter cloth over them. If you are feeling ambitious, it is even possible to glue fabric onto a square coffee table to give it an upholstered look.

For a startling modern look, primary colours and stripes give the desired effect. For this simple rectangular table-cloth and napkins you will need six colours in the same fabric, one colour will be for the tablecloth and the others make up the stripes and napkins. This is an ideal project for beginners.

Measure the length and width of the table. Decide on the drop, that is the length that the cloth hangs over the edge of the table (1). A drop of 8-12in (20-30cm) is average. Cut one piece of fabric to the required size plus 1 ½in (4cm) hem allowance all around. Lay the cloth flat, right side up, and measure for the decorative strips, beginning from corner to corner.

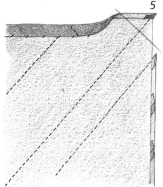

Cut out each strip, one from each of the five colours, to the required length and 3 ½in (9cm) wide. Join the strips if necessary with flat seams and press open (2).

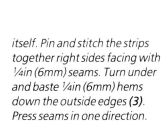

Lay the strips of fabric over the cloth in their final positions and pin in place (4). Make sure the two separate sections are 3in (8cm) apart along their length so that the green strip is an even width. Baste and machine stitch along the outside edges. Then machine stitch down each seam line between the colours. Trim the raw edges level with the edge of the tablecloth and turn under a double ¾in (2cm) hem all round. Mitre the corners (see page 179). Pin, baste and slipstitch the hem and corners in place (5). Remove all basting threads and press cloth.

Position the strips together in the desired sequence. For this design there will be two groups; purple and blue in one strip and yellow, orange and red in the other. The strip between blue and yellow is the green cloth itself. Pin and stitch the strips together right sides facing with ¼in (6mm) seams. Turn under and baste ¼in (6mm) hems down the outside edges (3). Press seams in one direction.

To make the napkins, decide on the size (see page 107) and cut out squares to this size plus ½in (12mm) allowance all around from each of the coloured fabrics. On each napkin, turn under a narrow ¼in (6mm) double hem around all edges, making neat folded corners. Pin and machine stitch the hems.

CIRCULAR CLOTH WITH POCKETS

On a hot summer's day, when the wind suddenly decides to blow, you might be glad of this highly original tablecloth which incorporates pockets in which to tuck table napkins. For a 36in (91cm) diameter table and four napkins, you will need 6 yards (5.5 metres) of a crisp, washable fabric and 1¼ yards (114cm) of ⅜in (9mm) elastic. If you live in a wayward climate, you could make the cloth from a lightweight waterproof fabric for patio use.

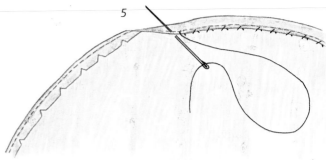

Measure the table across its width and add the required length of the overhang plus 1in (2.5cm) hem allowance at either side (1). Add these measurements together and make up a square of fabric. If a join is necessary, centre fabric on the table and attach an extra strip either side. Join and press seams open (2).

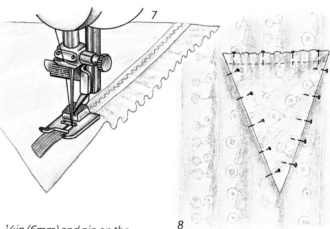

Turn in edge of cloth ¼in (6mm) to wrong side and press. Machine stitch close to fold and cut notches along edge; turn in ¾in (2cm) and hem neatly (5). With right sides facing, join pocket pieces, leaving an opening at the top (6). Clip corners, turn right side out, slipstitch opening and press. Cut a ⅜in (9mm) wide piece of elastic measuring ⅔ the length of the pocket top for each pocket. Fold under both ends

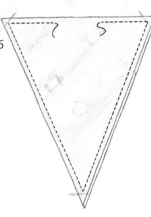

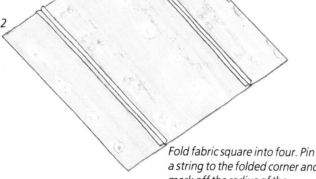

Fold fabric square into four. Pin a string to the folded corner and mark off the radius of the finished tablecloth plus hem allowance. Wind excess string around a soft pencil and trace outline lightly (3). Cut along marked line. Cut eight triangles for pockets, the top measuring a quarter the length of the cloth overhang and the sides twice that measurement (4).

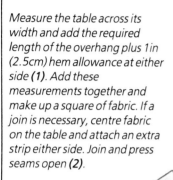

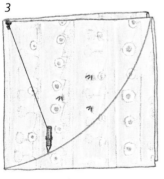

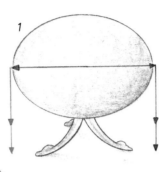

¼in (6mm) and pin on the pocket 1in (2.5cm) from the top. Machine along the centre of the stretched elastic with a zigzag stitch (7). Gather up the remaining pockets in the same way. Fold the cloth into quarters and mark the desired position of the pockets through all layers. Pin and baste pockets to the marked positions on the cloth and topstitch the ungathered sides close to the edge (8). Do not stretch the elastic when you sew on the pockets.

To make square table napkins, decide on the finished size and cut out four squares. Sizes generally range from no less than 12in (30cm) square up to 20in (51cm) with ¾in (2cm) allowances all around for hems. Turn in raw edges ¼in (6mm) and press. Turn in a further ½in (12mm) and topstitch close to the edge of the hem, neatening corners as you go. Press and fold napkins and tuck into pockets.

To make this tablecloth with its earthy appliqué motifs, you will need 4 yards (3.7 metres) of a mediumweight fabric for the cloth if your table is about 36in (91cm) across, pieces of coloured linen or cotton for the motifs, wadding and bias strips in a contrasting colour.

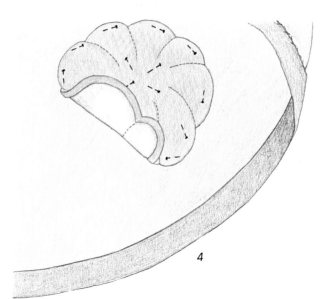

Decide on the diameter of the cloth. Join sections of fabric (see page 106) to make up a square, each side measuring the same as the diameter of the cloth. Fold into four (1) and with string, pencil and a pin mark the radius of the cloth (see page 106).

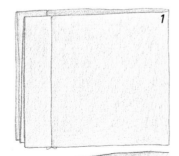

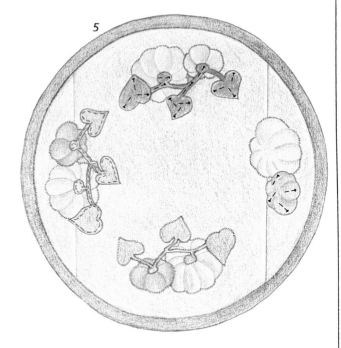

Cut out the circle of fabric through four thicknesses. Cut sufficient 6in (15cm) wide bias strips in a contrasting fabric to make up a length the circumference of the cloth. With right sides facing, pin to the edge of the cloth (2).

all around. Topstitch along marked quilting lines through both layers.
Trim ½in (12mm) from wadding all around pumpkin. Turn under a ½in (12mm) hem

to wrong side, pin and baste. Position and pin pumpkin to tablecloth (4) following the overall design (5). Slipstitch the folded edges of pumpkin to the cloth. Repeat until you have

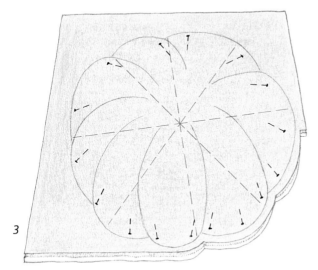

Stitch bias strip around cloth. Fold under a ½in (12mm) hem along the other edge and fold strip over to enclose the raw edges of cloth. Stitch folded edge of strip by hand to previous line of stitching.

Draw up appliqué motifs from pattern on page 171. To make pumpkin, pin and baste orange fabric to a layer of wadding, right side up (3). Mark in quilting lines and cut out shape leaving ½in (12mm) allowance

eight pumpkins in place. Cut out pattern pieces for stalks and leaves. Turn under ½in (12mm) all around outer edges of these pieces. Pin and baste to the cloth so that the stems match the centre of the

pumpkins. Slipstitch in place (5). Press cloth but avoid pressing the quilted motifs with wadding under them. Make a floor-length cloth in a darker shade and use the undercloth to highlight your appliqué work.

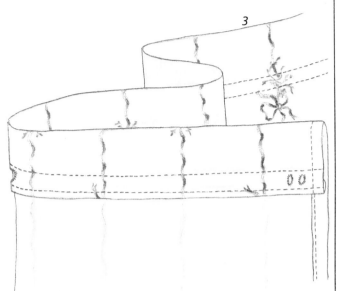

3

The deep fabric skirt hides an ordinary wooden table and makes an ideal piece of bedroom furniture. For an 18 × 36in (45 × 90cm) table top, you will need about 4½ yards (4.2 metres) of 36in (90cm) wide fabric, sufficient bias binding for the hem, seven hook eyes, curtain wire or strong cord and 1 yard (1 metre) of contrasting chintz for bows and ties.

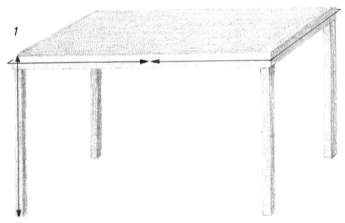

1

Cut fabric 1½ times the length around the table edge and the height from the floor plus 1¾in (4.5cm) (1). Neaten side edges of skirt with ½in (12mm) double hems. Fold fabric in half and mark positions of buttonholes with pins. Place pairs of buttonholes ½in (12mm) apart and ½in (12mm) down from top raw edge at

positions 1in (2.5cm) in from hemmed outer edges, at the centre front on fold, and the other four pairs should be spaced in between to match the corners of the table (2). The positions will depend on the size of your table but allowing for gathering up, each pair should be at the four corners and the centre front and back.

Encase the raw edge at the bottom in 1in (2.5cm) wide bias binding. Turn top edge to wrong side for ¼in (6mm) and press. Turn under a further 1½in (4cm), pin and stitch close

to first fold. Top stitch another seam ½in (12mm) above the buttonholes to form a casing (3). Do not sew over buttonholes.

Screw seven screw eyes into table rims, one at each corner, one at centre front and two either side of centre back (4). Press skirt. Loop one end of curtain wire through screw eye at centre back of table. Thread curtain wire through skirt casing. At every pair of buttonholes bring the wire out through the first hole, thread it through the hook and into the casing again through the other buttonhole. If you use cord, tie to back screw eyes and thread.

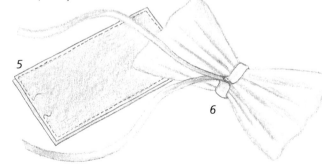

4

Make bows from two pieces of fabric measuring 3 × 7in (8 × 18cm). Machine stitch all around, leaving an opening at one end (5). Turn out and slipstitch opening. Make tie from bias strip 1½ × 24in (4 × 61cm). Wrap around bow (6),

and attach to skirt front ⅓ down from top.

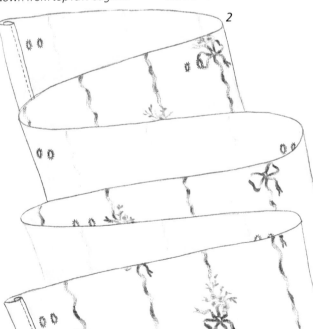

2

5

6

KIDNEY-SHAPED DRESSING-TABLE

Below these pretty skirts and the newly cut kidney-shaped wood and glass top lies an old office desk. The shaped top is screwed to the desk and the fabric hides the rest. You will need a crisp fabric, such as chintz, gathered heading tape, a curtain rail to go around the table top, and bias binding for the piping and the ruffle.

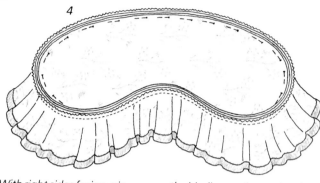

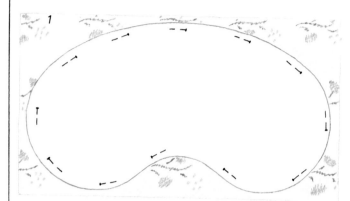

Make a paper template to fit the table top. Use it to cut out the fabric, adding ½in (12mm) allowance all around (**1**). Cut a 6in (15cm) wide strip of fabric 1½ times the length of the

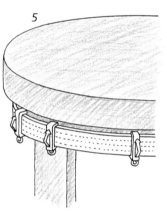

outer edge of the template. Join the strips to form a ring. Press seams open and run two rows of gathering stitch through the top of the ruffle. Stitch the bias binding to the other edge of the ruffle (see page 178) (**2**). Draw up the gathering threads so the ruffle fits evenly around the top of the kidney-shaped table. Make up a length of piped cord (see page 178) to fit around the table top. Pin it to the right side of ruffle, raw edges of piping

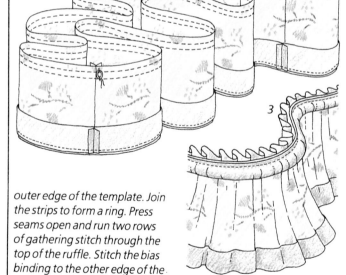

matching the raw edges of the top of the ruffle. Baste so that the gathers of the ruffle are held firmly in place (**3**).

With right sides facing, pin piped edge of ruffle around the top section, raw edges matching. Pin and stitch (**4**). Trim away seam allowance of

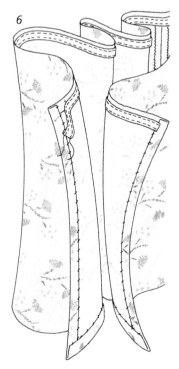

the binding on the cord so that there is less bulk in the seam. Neaten the raw edges of the ruffle, either with pinking shears or by oversewing.

Fit a flexible curtain track (**5**) around the top of the table, just beneath the rim, so that the ruffle will not interfere with the curtains. Use sections of track if necessary, butting ends up to one another at joins. For the skirt, measure the height of the table to the underside of the top. Cut fabric to this measurement, adding 2½in (6cm) for hems. The length should be 1½ times around the table top plus 2in (5cm) for hems.

Join the sections together to form a continuous strip for the skirt. Turn under a ½in (12mm) double hem down both side edges. Turn up and stitch a ½in (12mm) single hem around the lower edge. Turn down ½in (12mm) at the top and pin gathered heading tape over the hem (**6**). Baste and stitch in place. Draw up the heading tape so that the skirt hangs evenly around the table top. The opening should be at the front when you hang it from the curtain track. Pin up the lower hem just clear of the floor level. Hem stitch in place. Fit end stops to track where necessary. Fit ruffled top section. Have a sheet of plate glass with polished edges cut to fit. Lay the glass so the piping sits around its edge.

Asmart individual way to give your dated 1960s table a new lease of life is to cover it entirely with fabric. You will need enough fabric to cover the surface of your table, a glazed cotton would be ideal, a staple gun and some form of adhesive (read the manufacturer's recommendations first to check that it will not stain fabric).

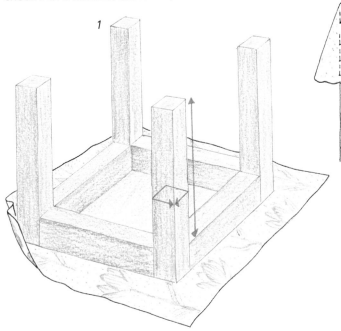

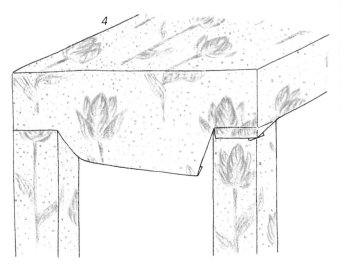

Position top cover, right side down, on table top. Pin excess fabric into pleats at each corner *(3)* so fabric fits table snuggly. Remove fabric from the table and stitch corner pleats. Trim excess fabric away and press. Cover table top with a light layer of adhesive and place fabric, right side up, onto it, matching seams to corners.

Lay the fabric face side down on the floor and position the table upside down onto it. Make sure the pattern is centred on the table and cut out a large enough piece for the fabric to cover the sides and tuck right under the table *(1)*. Measure around the table leg and its length adding 2in (5cm) on all sides. Cut out four pieces of fabric, making sure that the pattern matches on all four legs. Cover each leg in the same way. Beginning on the inside of the table, leave an equal allowance at the top and bottom and staple one raw edge of the fabric in place. Turn under raw edges along the other side and glue over the stapled edge. At the top, snip into the fabric at corners, glueing allowance under the table top and along the side. At the bottom, cut away corners and staple under the leg *(2)*.

At each leg, snip into fabric and turn under raw edges around the outside of the leg. Neaten and slipstitch to fabric covering the table leg *(4)*. Along the sides, fold the excess under the table top and staple or glue in place. To finish off, cut a square of felt and glue to the base of each leg.

115

TABLE TOP IDEAS

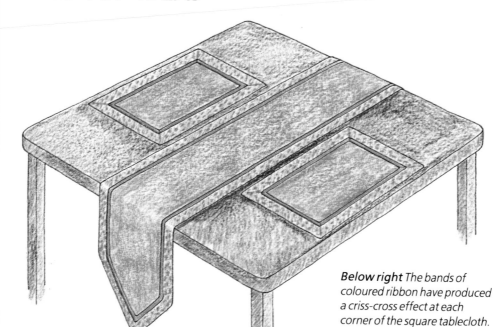

Left Interesting table mats and runners can be made from different shapes, colours and bindings. This is one of the simplest made out of plain fabric bound in a band of colour with a braid trim. For Christmas you could choose a red, green and white combination. Back the runner with nylon quilted fabric to protect the table or make the mats and runner from a ready-quilted, patterned fabric.

Below right The bands of coloured ribbon have produced a criss-cross effect at each corner of the square tablecloth. You use a lot of ribbon but you avoid having to mitre the corners many times. Topstitch the ribbons in place along both edges. Hem or face the edge of the tablecloth after the ribbons have been sewn on.

Below Tables often look prettier, richer and more interesting covered with several cloths. This round table has a plain circular cloth (see page 106) falling to the floor. It is then covered by two square cloths (see page 104) placed across one another. The edges of all three cloths are decorated with two bands of coloured bias binding topstitched in place at equal distances from the outer edges of each cloth. You could also use a printed fabric border, possibly to match the wallpaper or the other soft furnishings in the room.

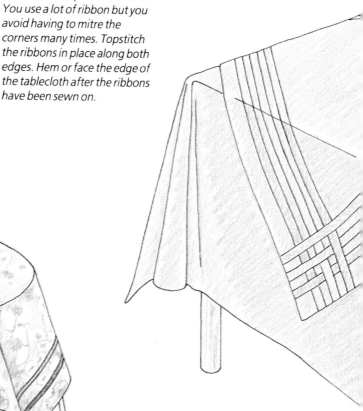

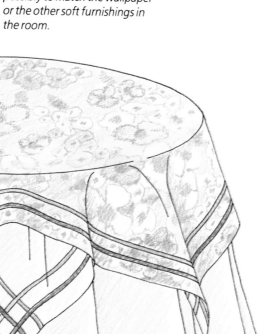

Right *A cloth with a complicated appliqué edging looks at its best shown off against a full-length circular cloth. Here are two appliqué designs; the one using fruit shapes is cut as a square and the other with flower shapes is a circular cloth. Apply the shapes (see pages 48 and 150) and then cut away excess fabric. Appliqué work does take time, but properly planned and finished it has a lasting appeal.*

Below *A fitted circular tablecloth looks more dressy and is ideal for a bedroom. The ruffled skirt is made of lace overlaid on a plain coloured lining. The edge of the table is defined by piping covered in the matching lining fabric. The method is as for the kidney-shaped dressing-table on page 112.*

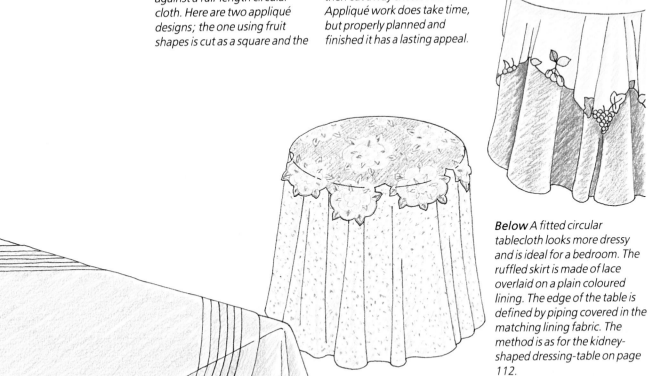

5

SWEET DREAMS

No other room in the house offers quite the scope for using fabric as the bedroom. Practically everything in it can be covered with fabric, and you can inject a great deal of style simply in the manner in which you dress your bed. A simple geometric quilt and matching pillow may be all you need, or make your own four-poster with curtain poles and a canopy attached to the ceiling. The bedspread, valance and cushions can all be made up in fabrics which combine well with the new 'look'.

SERRATED-EDGED PILLOWCASE

Luxurious bed linen can be very expensive but you can make your own distinctive design in the colour and style of your choice. The serrated-edged pillowcase design has a tailored timelessness and it costs only the price of the sheeting fabric, thread and a zip. The serrated edge has the advantage of all geometric shapes in keeping a crisp, fresh appearance. We have chosen to use a zip in this pillowcase so that the shape of the pillow is firmly held and it can be left uncovered on the bed. You will need 2¾ yards (2.5 metres) of fabric for each pillowcase and a zip. Sheeting fabric with a non-iron finish is the best to use; it usually comes in 45in (115cm) widths or wider.

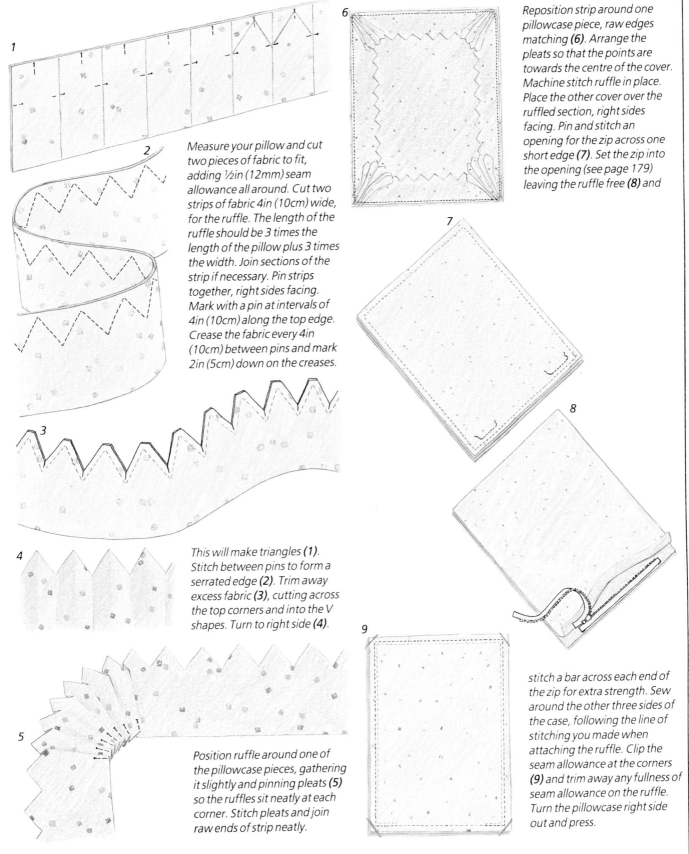

1

2

Measure your pillow and cut two pieces of fabric to fit, adding ½in (12mm) seam allowance all around. Cut two strips of fabric 4in (10cm) wide, for the ruffle. The length of the ruffle should be 3 times the length of the pillow plus 3 times the width. Join sections of the strip if necessary. Pin strips together, right sides facing. Mark with a pin at intervals of 4in (10cm) along the top edge. Crease the fabric every 4in (10cm) between pins and mark 2in (5cm) down on the creases.

3

4

This will make triangles *(1)*. Stitch between pins to form a serrated edge *(2)*. Trim away excess fabric *(3)*, cutting across the top corners and into the V shapes. Turn to right side *(4)*.

5

Position ruffle around one of the pillowcase pieces, gathering it slightly and pinning pleats *(5)* so the ruffles sit neatly at each corner. Stitch pleats and join raw ends of strip neatly.

6

Reposition strip around one pillowcase piece, raw edges matching *(6)*. Arrange the pleats so that the points are towards the centre of the cover. Machine stitch ruffle in place. Place the other cover over the ruffled section, right sides facing. Pin and stitch an opening for the zip across one short edge *(7)*. Set the zip into the opening (see page 179) leaving the ruffle free *(8)* and

7

8

9

stitch a bar across each end of the zip for extra strength. Sew around the other three sides of the case, following the line of stitching you made when attaching the ruffle. Clip the seam allowance at the corners *(9)* and trim away any fullness of seam allowance on the ruffle. Turn the pillowcase right side out and press.

BEDSPREAD, VALANCE AND HEADBOARD

In most bedrooms, the bed occupies a central position and anything between one-third and one-half of the room's total floor area. If you revamp the bedspread and valance and make a headboard you will give the room a new lease of life. This idea is an old favourite, perhaps because it is easy to execute and comfortable to live with.

The tailored, box-pleated valance is more practical than the ruffled variety, especially if you use sheets and blankets on the bed. A ruffled valance tends to get tucked in with the bedclothes. The headboard is made from foam shapes and they can be hung by loops slid onto a pole fixed horizontally to the wall above the bed. If you prefer a more elaborate headboard, then you can make a plywood shape, surround it with wadding and make a pillowcase style of cover. For this project you will need fabric for the headboard, bedspread and valance and contrasting bias strip and cord for the piping around the headboard, a foam shape for the headboard, a zip, a decorative pole from which to hang it, interfacing and lining for the bedspread and a cheap fabric for the central panel of the valance.

To make the headboard, measure the bed and calculate the size (see page 181). Here there are two equal-sized headboards. Cut two pieces of foam to the required size. Cut out a front and back for the cover and the welt sections; one of the welt sections should be 1in (2.5cm) wider to take the zip. Allow for seam allowances

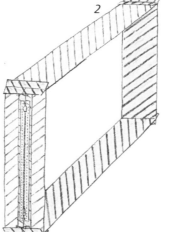

all around. Stitch the zip into the welt as described on pages 70-71 (1). This zip need not go round the corners.

Pin and stitch the four welt pieces together with flat fell seams (2). Cut 2in (5cm) wide strips of fabric on the bias (see page 178) and join together to make a strip long enough to go around the entire welt twice. Make piping with this bias strip and pin and baste along its length (see page 178). Pin and baste piping around the top and bottom of the welt, ½in (12mm) in from the raw edges.

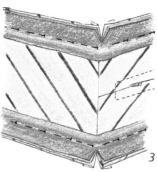

Join ends of piping together by overlapping them and stitching across the cords through all layers. Snip into the piping to ease it around the corners (3).

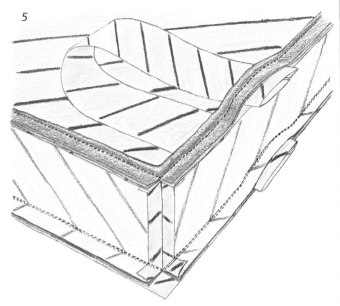

5

Position one piece of the headboard cover, right sides facing, to the piped welt. Pin and machine stitch, catching in one side of the loops *(5)*. Open the zip and pin and stitch the other cover in place *(6)*. Trim and turn to right side. Insert foam pad and close zip. Hang from decorative pole secured above the bed.

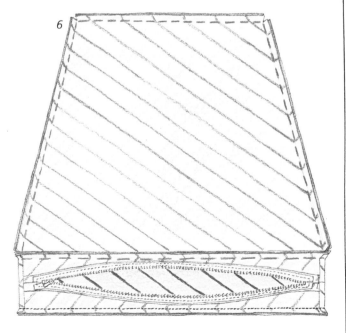

6

To make the fabric loops, make up a strip of fabric 44in (111cm) long by 8in (20cm) wide and fold in half lengthwise with right sides facing. Sew along the long edge ½in (12mm) from the raw edges. Turn out and press *(4)*. Cut strip into four equal lengths for the loops. Mark the centre of one long side of welt. Position one loop on either side of this point and two on the outer edges. Slot the end of each loop between piping and welt, unpicking the basting thread at this point *(5)*.

4

To estimate the amount of fabric for the bedspread, measure the bed (see page 181) with all the usual bedclothes in place. Cut a length of fabric the width of the bed top and pin and stitch two equal strips down either side equal to the desired overhang plus hem allowance. Use flat fell seams to join.

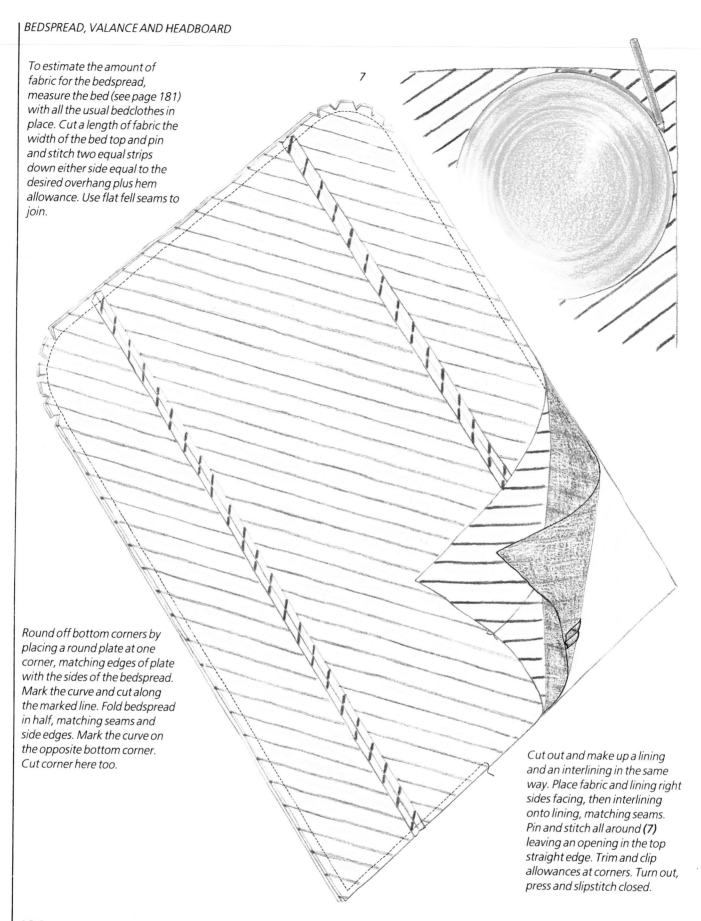

7

Round off bottom corners by placing a round plate at one corner, matching edges of plate with the sides of the bedspread. Mark the curve and cut along the marked line. Fold bedspread in half, matching seams and side edges. Mark the curve on the opposite bottom corner. Cut corner here too.

Cut out and make up a lining and an interlining in the same way. Place fabric and lining right sides facing, then interlining onto lining, matching seams. Pin and stitch all around (7) leaving an opening in the top straight edge. Trim and clip allowances at corners. Turn out, press and slipstitch closed.

Remove mattress and measure the bed base. For valance top, cut two 9in (23cm) wide strips of valance fabric, the length of the base plus 1in (2.5cm) allowances, and one strip 9in (23cm) wide the width of the bed plus 2in (5cm). Cut one central panel 15¾in (40cm) narrower than the bed base and 8in (20cm) shorter, from a cheap fabric. For valance skirt, cut two strips for the length of the bed and one for the width, and two 16in (40cm) inserts for the pleats plus 4in (10cm). You can economize this way by having a frame of valance fabric around the central rectangle of cheap fabric (8) which will not be seen, even when the bedspread is not on the bed.

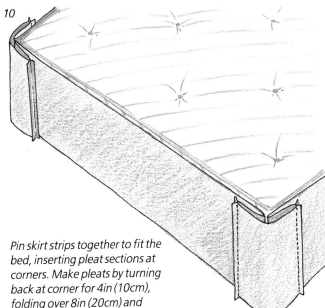

10

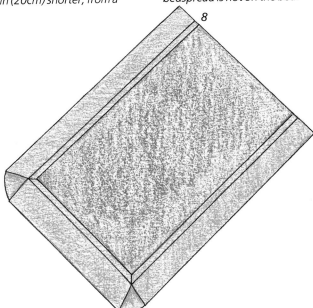

8

Pin skirt strips together to fit the bed, inserting pleat sections at corners. Make pleats by turning back at corner for 4in (10cm), folding over 8in (20cm) and then 4in (10cm) back to corner. At corners, if possible the seams should lie along the fold of the pleat (10). Baste and stitch skirt sections together. Lay central panel right side down on the bed base. Position valance skirt to border, matching raw edges at top and border corners with centre of pleats. Pin and stitch. Clip corners.

At top edge, turn under a double ½in (12mm) hem across valance border and central panel. Pin and stitch in place. Lay valance over bed base and check for length. Turn up ½in (12mm) and then the necessary amount to bring the skirt just off the floor. Pin and stitch valance hem in place (11).

Pin and stitch border pieces around central panel up to corner points. Mitre border at corners (see page 178) and sew to panel (9). Press seams open. Lay central panel with border on base to check for fit. It should overhang the edges by ½in (12mm) seam allowance

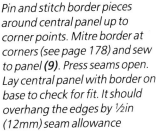

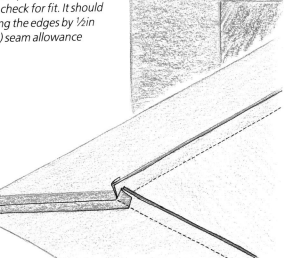

9

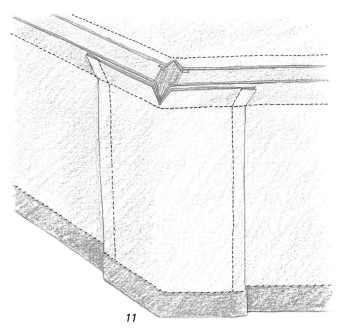

11

Stencilling a pattern onto an inexpensive cotton bedspread yields individual and pretty results. The slightly curved design of flowers and leaves is repeated several times around the inside of a circle. On the headboard it is repeated within a semi-circle (for instructions on making a headboard see page 123). You can scale the stencil pattern up or down depending on the width of your bed, so it is wise to make up a paper pattern first and then plan the positions of your stencilled pattern and the number of repeats before you apply the paint. Fabric paints are now well tested and keep their colours after washing, provided you apply them according to the manufacturer's instructions. You will need enough cotton or fabric of your choice to cover the bed, lining fabric – muslin or a wide sheeting fabric would do – wadding, bias binding, fabric paints and stiff paper to make the stencil.

Measure your bed (see page 181) and from your chosen fabric cut out two lengths and cut one in half lengthwise. Pin and stitch together the narrow strips to either side of the central strip (see page 124) and round off the corners (1). Cut out and make up the lining in the same way.

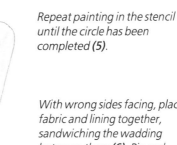

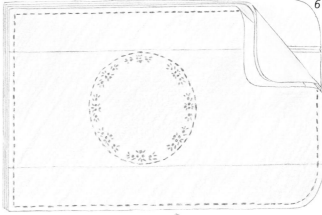

Cut out two lengths of wadding to size. Place with long edges butting together. Herringbone stitch the long edges together (2). Place top fabric over the bed with pillows only in place and decide on the position of the central circle. Mark the centre point of the circle.

Tie a length of string around the pointed end of a soft pencil. Place a pin at the central point of the design and wind the other end of the string around it to the desired radius of the circle. Keeping the string taut, mark a circle on the fabric (3). Cut a circle of paper to the same size and mark out the overall design from the template on

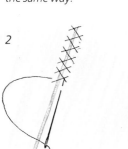

page 172, noting the distances between each pattern repeat. Trace the stencil onto stiff paper. Place the paper on a cutting board so as not to damage your working surface. Using a sharp craft knife cut out the stencil holes (4). With the bedspread laid out flat, place the stencil on the right side of the fabric, inside the marked circle, making sure it corresponds with your paper plan in relation to the head and bottom of the bed. Hold the stencil firmly in place with scotch tape. Using a stencil brush and fabric paints, colour in each part of the design. Leave to dry, then carefully lift off the stencil. Using a fine artist's paintbrush, paint in any jagged or heavy lines by hand.

Repeat painting in the stencil until the circle has been completed (5).

With wrong sides facing, place fabric and lining together, sandwiching the wadding between them (6). Pin and baste around the outer edges and around the central circle, following the marked pencil line. Stitch around outer edges through all layers and stitch around the central circle to give a quilted effect. Trim wadding back to stitching line. Measure around all outer edges and make up two lengths of bias binding to this length plus 3in (8cm) allowance.

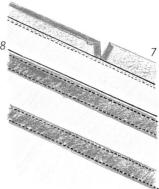

Unfold one edge of the binding and press open. Pin this right side of binding to the wrong side of bedspread all around the outside edges. Turn back and overlap short ends of bias binding. Stitch through crease line of binding (7). Press binding over outer edge to the right side of bedspread. Mitre the top corners and pin and topstitch in place with thread of the same colour as the binding. Fold other length of bias binding in half lengthwise and pin to bedspread at an equal distance from the first strip of binding. Fold binding into mitres at top

corners and ease around the curved edges at the bottom. Topstitch in place along both edges (8).

FOUR-POSTER BED

For this dainty four-poster bed you will need muslin, or any washable fabric that gathers up well and isn't heavy, for the canopy, broderie anglaise in two widths for the ruffle, a contrast fabric for the tiny ruffle, four long and four shorter curtain wires or lengths of strong cord and screw eyes.

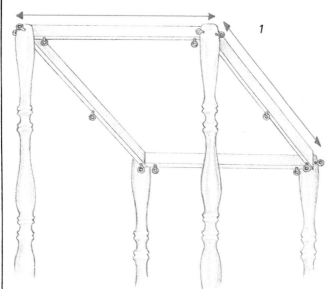

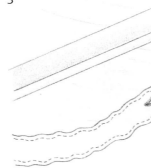

The canopy is held in place by four curtain wires running through casings and fitted down all sides of the bed under the top struts. The ruffle is held in place by four lengths of curtain wire fitted around the top of the frame. Therefore you will need to fix screw eyes along the sides and the underside of the frame to hold these curtain wires. You can use strong cord instead of the curtain wires. Cut to length and tie firmly to the screw eyes at either end. Measure the width and length of the frame (1) at the outer edges of the top struts. For the canopy cut a rectangle 1½ times the length of the bed by the width plus an allowance of 2in (5cm) all around. Join sections of fabric as necessary.

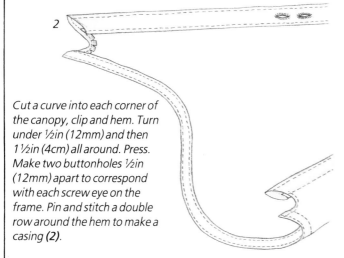

Cut a curve into each corner of the canopy, clip and hem. Turn under ½in (12mm) and then 1½in (4cm) all around. Press. Make two buttonholes ½in (12mm) apart to correspond with each screw eye on the frame. Pin and stitch a double row around the hem to make a casing (2).

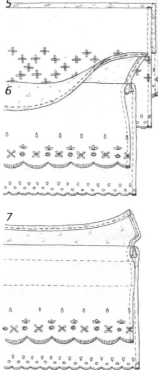

Cut four lengths of broderie anglaise, 15in (40cm) wide by 1½ times around the post. Make a ¼in (6mm) double hem down sides. Turn under ¼in (6mm), then 1½in (4cm) to make a casing around the top raw edge. Thread a cord through the casing and tie the broderie anglaise 'skirt' tightly around each post (4). This will disguise the top of the posts when looked at from inside the four-poster bed.

For the ruffle, use two lengths of broderie anglaise, one 15in (40cm) wide, the other 12in

Thread curtain wire or cord through the casing and out through buttonhole and through the screw eye (3), gathering the fullness as you go. Hook ends of wire onto screw eyes or tie cord at corners. Repeat for other three sides.

(30cm) wide, and a contrast strip 5in (10cm) wide to the length of 1½ times right around the frame. Hem one long edge of the contrast strip. Join short ends of each strip to make three large loops. Lay the three strips together, raw edges aligned, right sides up, the 12in (30cm) strip on the bottom, then the contrast strip, then the widest strip. Pin, baste and stitch ½in (12mm) from the raw edges (5). Turn widest strip to back (6), press and make a double row of stitching through layers of broderie anglaise to make a casing (7). Make buttonholes by hand in the casing to correspond to the screw eyes on the side of the frame. Use four lengths of curtain wire or cord and thread up as for canopy.

PATCHWORK QUILT

This elegant, understated patchwork quilt is made entirely by machine and is designed to use just a few carefully chosen colours and patterns placed in a strict lattice design. You will need six fabrics in different patterns and tones for the patchwork, templates (see page 170), wadding, a backing fabric and bias strips for the bound edge.

The patchwork bedspread is made up of four different elements. Each is made up separately and then joined. Following the key *(1)*:

a = large patchwork squares made up of triangles (striped fabric), diamonds (patterned fabric), small squares (dark) and strips (pale) *(2)*. Make 4 whole squares and 8 half squares.

b = smaller patchwork squares, made up of squares of plain fabric in three shades *(9)*. Make 24 whole squares, and 16 half squares.

c = wide strips of pale fabric. You will need 32.

d = the border, made up of small squares in the same colours as *b (10)*.

1

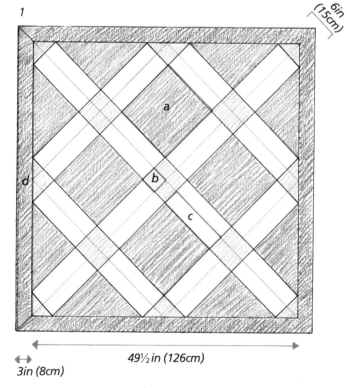

3in (8cm)

49½ in (126cm)

6in (15cm)

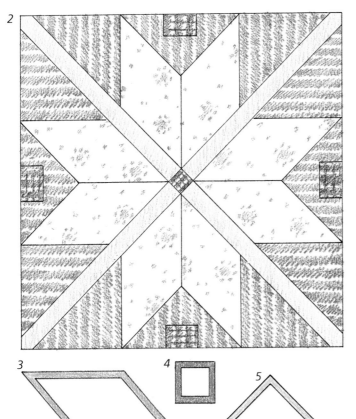

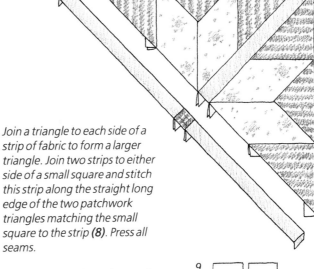

Join a triangle to each side of a strip of fabric to form a larger triangle. Join two strips to either side of a small square and stitch this strip along the straight long edge of the two patchwork triangles matching the small square to the strip **(8)**. Press all seams.

Turn under ¼in (6mm) around three edges of remaining small squares. Appliqué small squares to the centre of each outside edge, stitching in place by hand. Stitch around three sides only.

For each of the small patchwork squares **b**, cut out one 1¾in (4.5cm) dark square and four each of the same size in the mid and light tone. Join them with the dark square in the centre and the mid tone at the four corners **(9)**.

Cut 32 strips of pale fabric 3¾ × 12½in (9.5 × 32cm) **c**. Join small squares to each end of each of 16 of the strips, joining half squares to strips where they meet the edge of the quilt. Join pairs of strips to form wider strips, then join sides of squares **b** to form a set of strips which will form the diagonals. Join remaining 16 strips to each side of large patchwork squares. Join free edges of strips, then join wide strips (of **a** and **b**) between diagonal strips (of **b** and **c**).

To make the border **d**, cut 1¾in (4.5cm) squares of fabric in the light, dark and mid tones. Make up squares as shown **(10)**. Join

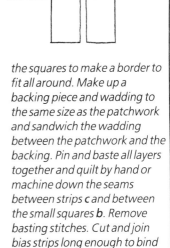

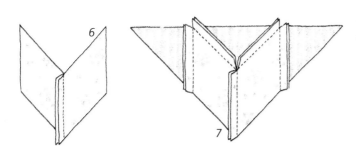

Start with the large squares **a** **(2)**. Choose four contrasting fabrics. Make the templates (see page 170) **(3,4,5)** from heavy card. The outer edge on the template represents the cutting line. The seam allowance is ¼in (6mm). The sharp angles should should be 45°. For each square, cut eight diamonds, twelve triangles and five squares. Cut four strips of fabric 9 × 1¾in (23 × 4.5cm). Join the sections

by machine. First join pairs of diamonds along one edge **(6)** then set a triangle into the angle formed. Add a triangle on each side to make a patchwork triangle roughly one-quarter the size of the finished square. Press the seams together and clip excess fabric from the corners to enable the seam allowance to lie flat **(7)**.

the squares to make a border to fit all around. Make up a backing piece and wadding to the same size as the patchwork and sandwich the wadding between the patchwork and the backing. Pin and baste all layers together and quilt by hand or machine down the seams between strips **c** and between the small squares **b**. Remove basting stitches. Cut and join bias strips long enough to bind the edge of the quilt (see page 178).

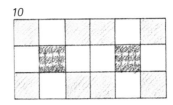

LOG CABIN QUILT

Log cabin patchwork can yield intricate and interesting three-dimensional results, especially if you make each square exactly the same. To work out a satisfying design, make up a sample square and place two mirrors at right angles to it. This will show you what the same squares will look like when sewn together. You will need dark- and light-coloured and patterned strips of fabric, squares for the centre, plain cotton for the foundation squares, interlining or wadding and backing.

1

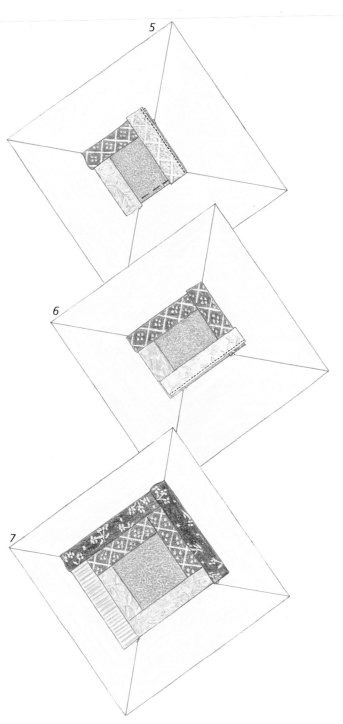

5

6

7

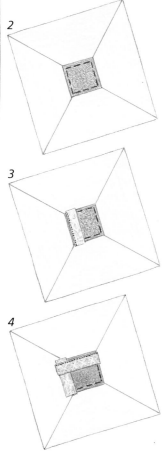

2

3

4

For each square of patchwork **(1)**, cut out one foundation square from plain cotton to the required size – 12in (30cm) squares are a good size. Decide on the width of your strips; 1in (2.5cm) is average with ¼in (6mm) seam allowances, making 1½in (4cm) wide strips. You will need equal numbers of dark and light strips. You also need a central square for each piece, 2in (5cm) square in size. Draw two lines from corner to corner on the foundation square and place the central square over the intersection. Pin and baste around the outer edge **(2)**. Pin and machine stitch the first light strip to one edge of the central square **(3)**, with right sides facing and making a ¼in (6mm) seam. Press flat against the foundation square and pin and stitch a dark-coloured strip along the adjacent side of the central square, overlapping the first strip at one end **(4)**. Press flat as before. Then pin and stitch another dark-coloured strip to

the third side of the central square **(5)**, each time overlapping the previous strip. Keep working around the square in this way, with light strips on one half and dark on the other **(6,7)**. When you reach the edge of the foundation square, baste around the edges

to hold strips flat. Repeat to make up more squares in this way. Pin and stitch the squares together to make up the bedspread. Plan first, using the light and dark sides to good effect. Make up the bedspread (see page 124).

MOSES BASKET

For this average-sized Moses basket, you will need 3 yards (2.75 metres) of 36in (91cm) wide main fabric, 2 yards (1.8 metres) each of lining or a matching fabric as shown here and wadding, six press studs, 80in (205cm) ribbon to tie the basket lining in place, 4½ yards (4 metres) of 1in (2.5cm) bias binding and 2 yards (1.8 metres) of 2½in (6cm) bias strips.

4

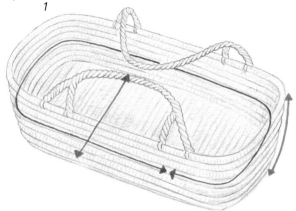

1

Measure circumference of basket at widest point and add 3in (8cm) allowance. Measure the depth and add 4in (10cm) **(1)**. Cut the side strip to this size from fabric, wadding and lining. With main fabric right side down, lay the wadding and then the lining on to it. Pin and

baste along both long edges and with right sides facing join short ends in a flat seam **(2)**. Make a paper pattern for the basket bottom, and cut out fabric, wadding and lining from this pattern allowing ½in (12mm) all around. Baste together around edges. Make

notches on one long edge of side piece and pin and baste to bottom with right sides facing. Stitch in place **(3)**.

Drop the lining into the basket and mark the position of the handles with pins. Cut away holes through all layers to allow a good fit around handles. Neaten raw edges with 2½in (6cm) bias strips of fabric around holes and between them on the straight edges **(4)**. Cut strip for ruffle 1½ times the circumference in length plus 4in (10cm) and ⅓ the depth of the basket plus 2in (5cm). Cut strip

in half and neaten four short ends with a ½in (12mm) double hem. Enclose one long raw edge with 1in (2.5cm) wide bias binding (see page 178). Run two lines of gathering stitches through the other long edge and pull up to fit half the basket. Each ruffle should start at a handle edge and extend around to the handle edge diagonally opposite. The ruffle piece that covers the area between the handles will be bound to hold the gathers. With right sides facing, pin, baste and stitch ruffle sections to basket lining **(5)**.

2

3

5

6

Bind raw edges of ruffle to hold gathers with 2½in (6cm) bias strips. Attach four 20in (51cm) lengths of ribbon tied into bows to ruffle at handles. Sew three press studs onto binding between handles and onto ruffle opposite (6). You can stitch a piece of elastic along the seam line where the ruffle is joined to the lining for a secure fit. Cut the elastic ⅔ the length to be elasticated and sew with a zigzag stitch on your machine (see page 106).

To make the coverlet, cut a paper pattern to fit inside the basket, round off the corners evenly and cut out one piece

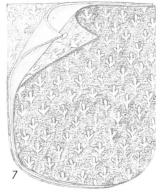

each of fabric, wadding and lining (7). With right sides facing, pin and stitch lining to fabric and wadding along straight edge. Fold lining to inside, topstitch raw curved edges together and measure

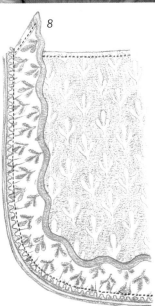

8

around curved edge. Cut a strip 1½ times this length for the ruffle. Make the ruffle as before, with wrong sides facing, pin and stitch to coverlet (8). Press seam allowance towards ruffle and cover the raw edges with a strip of 1in (2.5cm) bias binding. Pin and topstitch (9).

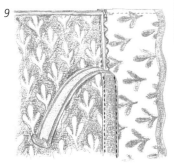

9

BED-LINEN IDEAS

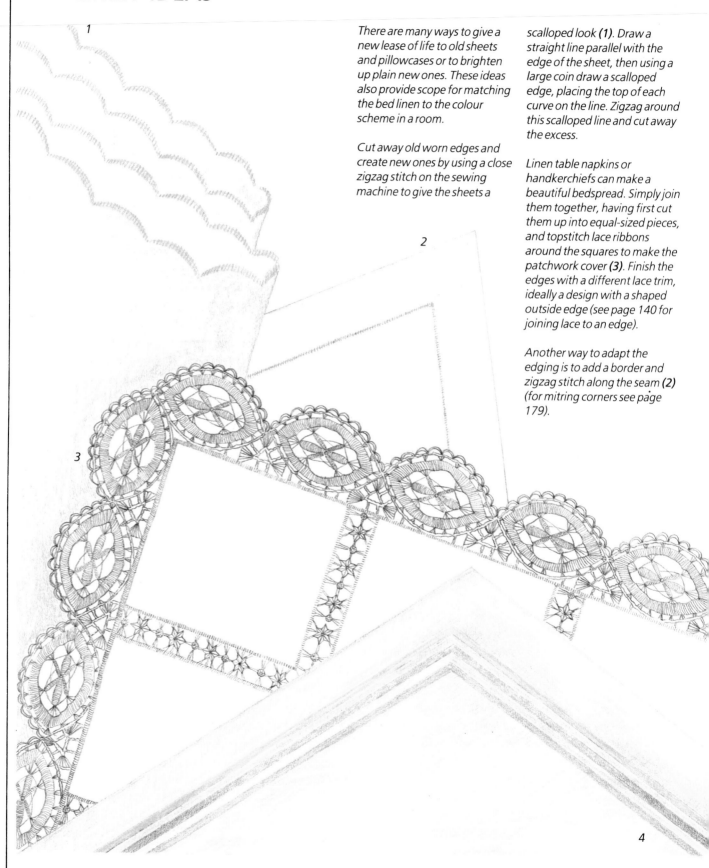

There are many ways to give a new lease of life to old sheets and pillowcases or to brighten up plain new ones. These ideas also provide scope for matching the bed linen to the colour scheme in a room.

Cut away old worn edges and create new ones by using a close zigzag stitch on the sewing machine to give the sheets a scalloped look (**1**). Draw a straight line parallel with the edge of the sheet, then using a large coin draw a scalloped edge, placing the top of each curve on the line. Zigzag around this scalloped line and cut away the excess.

Linen table napkins or handkerchiefs can make a beautiful bedspread. Simply join them together, having first cut them up into equal-sized pieces, and topstitch lace ribbons around the squares to make the patchwork cover (**3**). Finish the edges with a different lace trim, ideally a design with a shaped outside edge (see page 140 for joining lace to an edge).

Another way to adapt the edging is to add a border and zigzag stitch along the seam (**2**) (for mitring corners see page 179).

Yellow, blue and green bands of ribbon **(4)** are used to match the linen to a wallpaper in the same colour combination. Leave about ¼in (6mm) gap between the rows of topstitched ribbon. It is a good idea to rule lines first, and pin and baste the ribbons in place. This guarantees that the lines of ribbon will be straight and crisp. For a bedspread you can interweave the ribbons at the corners **(7)**. Place the ribbons at least 1in (2.5cm) apart and choose a slightly heavier ribbon. You will need a lot of ribbon for this idea.

A ruffle never fails to appeal if used in the appropriate surroundings. You can buy ready-made ruffles of broderie anglaise or lace and this saves a lot of effort **(5)**. Ruffles are merely gathered on around a corner, so you don't have to mitre. Use layers of ruffles, either the same width or different widths and, if using lace, combine it with a darker coloured, lightweight fabric to show up the lace pattern.

The least expensive ruffle is made from sheeting fabric, cut into strips, folded lengthwise and gathered along the raw edges. To give the pillowcase a special finish, edge the bottom of the ruffle with a plain or patterned ribbon and sew tiny bows at regular intervals along the ribbon **(6)**. To achieve these changes on your pillowcases you will have to unpick the long seams so that you can lay the case out flat and do the sewing by machine. You can cheer up plain coloured pillowcases by sewing several bands of ribbon or coloured bias binding to the outside edges, or place a thin layer of wadding under the ribbons for a textured effect.

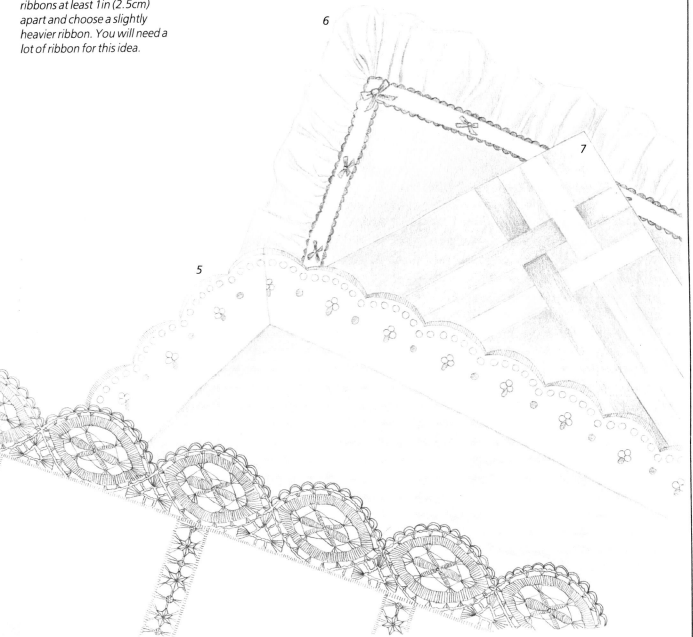

6

7

5

6
FINISHING TOUCHES

Just like homemade cookies or pâté, it is often those very special small touches – a lamp shade carefully made to co-ordinate with colours in a rug, or a pot-pourri bag inside the guest room drawer designed to match the curtains – which make a house look especially cherished. Here are some ideas for you to copy or adapt, if not for your own house, then for friends. The smaller items make particularly welcome presents.

LACE LAMPSHADE

This simple lampshade is made out of a circle of fabric, edged with lace and finished off with drops of pearls. It is designed to be decorative rather than functional and, for safety's sake, you should combine it with a low-voltage lamp bulb and choose a frame that allows for a minimum gap of 4in (10cm) between the top of the bulb and the fabric. You will need about 1 yard (1 metre) of fabric, such as broderie anglaise or lace, lace trimming, pearl droplets, a frame and ½in (12mm) tape.

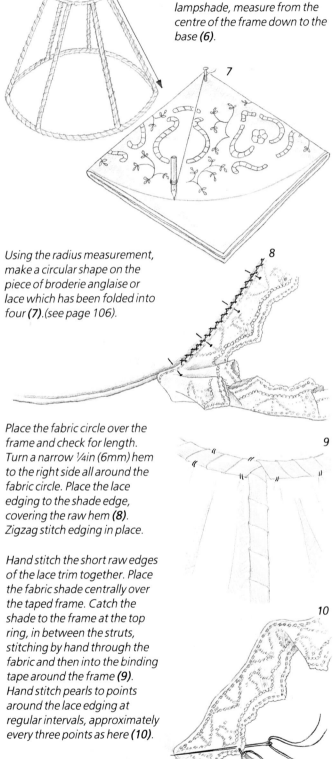

To find the radius of the lampshade, measure from the centre of the frame down to the base (6).

To tape the lampshade frame, use ½in (12mm) wide cotton tape. For each strut you will need tape 1½ times the length of the strut. Secure the tape in a ball with a rubber band so it won't get twisted up. Take the first length, fold it over the top ring and around the strut, tucking in the end (1). Continue to wind the tape at an acute angle, tightly and smoothly, stretching it as you wind. At the bottom, take the tape over the bottom ring, round the strut and the tape. Pull it tight to form a knot (2).

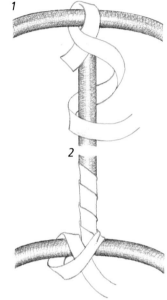

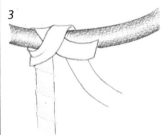

Using the radius measurement, make a circular shape on the piece of broderie anglaise or lace which has been folded into four (7).(see page 106).

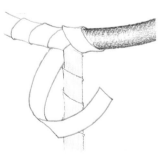

Make a figure-of-eight when you reach a taped strut position (4&5).

Repeat the taping on each strut. Tape around the rings (3), measuring the circumference of each ring and cutting twice the length of tape.

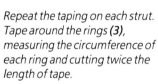

Place the fabric circle over the frame and check for length. Turn a narrow ¼in (6mm) hem to the right side all around the fabric circle. Place the lace edging to the shade edge, covering the raw hem (8). Zigzag stitch edging in place.

Hand stitch the short raw edges of the lace trim together. Place the fabric shade centrally over the taped frame. Catch the shade to the frame at the top ring, in between the struts, stitching by hand through the fabric and then into the binding tape around the frame (9). Hand stitch pearls to points around the lace edging at regular intervals, approximately every three points as here (10).

To finish off, fold under ¼in (6mm) of the tape and stitch this hem neatly by hand to the outside of the bound strut or ring.

BEDSIDE TABLE ACCESSORIES

So often it is the small detail that catches the eye and gives a finishing touch to the colour and style of a room. This is especially appreciated if the items are handmade, and in fabric to match your colour scheme. The lampshade is done by hand, and if you already have a fabric shade, you could treat it as the lining and apply the pleated cover to it. For the lampshade you need 1 yard (1 metre) of lining and 3 yards (2.75 metres) of fabric, a coolie-shaped frame, tape for the frame and fabric for binding. Changing the colour of your lampshades is an easy way to change the look of your room at night. For instance, if you want a warm glow, choose an apricot lining and a cover fabric in tones of apricot and pink.

The tissue box is quick and easy to make and the semicircular sponge bag could also be used to store jewelry or make-up. The tiny sachet, which is a simple sandwich of fabric and wadding, would make a pretty lavender bag to scent drawers. They can each be made from ½ yard (45cm) offcuts of fabric and you need ribbons and wadding, and for the sponge bag about ½ yard (45cm) of waterproof lining and 1 yard (1 metre) of 2¼in (6cm) binding.

Tissue box Measure the panels: one is from one side of the opening to the other by the length of the box. The second panel is the width of the box by the length around it from one end of the opening to the other *(1)*. Cut two pieces of fabric for each panel, adding ½in (12mm) seam allowance all around. Cut four ties, 1½ × 12in (4 × 30cm), and make up.

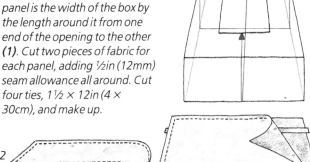

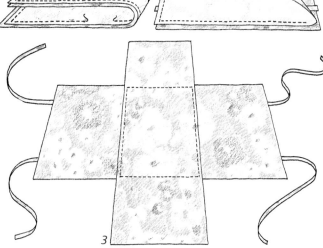

With right sides facing, stitch fabric pieces together all around edges, leaving a 4in (10cm) opening in each. Catch ties into shorter edge of large panel *(2)*. Turn right side out, press and slipstitch openings.

Lay narrow panel on top of the larger panel. Pin, baste and stitch all around the rectangular base where the fabric overlaps, through all layers *(3)*. Press again and wrap around box. Tie to hold in place.

Perfumed sachet Make up a muslin sachet and fill it with dried lavender *(4)*. Cut two pieces of wadding, same size as muslin sachet and two pieces of fabric, 1½in (4cm) larger all around than sachet. Cut an 8in (20cm) length of ribbon. Sandwich the sachet between the wadding and fabric. Pin and baste, catching ribbon in one side *(5)*. Using a closed-up zigzag stitch, stitch ¼in (6mm) and 1in (2.5cm) from the raw edges. Trim away raw edges *(6)*.

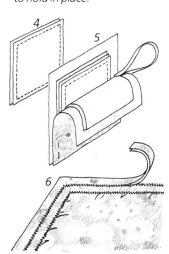

Sponge bag Cut two circles of fabric 12in (30cm) in diameter and two circles of waterproof lining. Cut a piece of wadding at least 12½in (32cm) square *(7)*. Cut one piece of fabric and one of lining in half to form the semi-circles for the pockets. Baste wadding to top fabric to hold in place. Pin waterproof lining circle to back and pin around the edge.

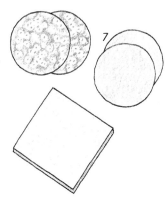

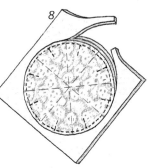

Stitch through all three layers close to the edge of the circle. Trim away excess wadding close to stitching *(8)*. If you want to quilt the bag, quilt through wadding and fabric only. If you pierce the lining it will not be waterproof.

Cut a selection of ribbons in varying widths and colours. Pin across the circle. Avoid pinning through the lining. Slipstitch the ribbons in place by hand *(9)*.

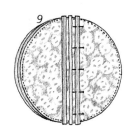

For the pockets, take one semi-circle of fabric and one of lining. Pin together around edges, right sides facing outwards. Use a 12in (30cm) strip of bias binding or bias cut fabric to bind the straight edges together *(10)*. Repeat for the second pocket.

Position the pockets on the circle, with lined sides facing. The bound edges of the pockets should run at right angles to the ribbon trimming on the other side of the circle. Pin and baste pockets in place, then stitch all around outer edge of the circle, through all layers *(11)*.

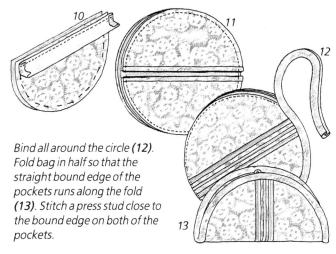

Bind all around the circle *(12)*. Fold bag in half so that the straight bound edge of the pockets runs along the fold *(13)*. Stitch a press stud close to the bound edge on both of the pockets.

143

PLEATED COOLIE-SHAPED SHADE

First you must tape the basic coolie-shaped frame (1). This will give you something to stitch the fabric lining and cover to. Wrap the tape evenly around the frame to give a smooth finish and stitch the ends in place so that it does not unravel (see pages 140-141). Use a pale lining to reflect light.

Slip the lining inside the frame with the right side facing inwards and pin to the top and bottom rings so that the lining is tightly stretched around the inside of the frame. Line the seams up with the side struts. Pin at right angles to the rings (4), through the tapes binding the frame. Fold excess lining back over to the outside of the frame around the top and bottom rings. Stitch the lining to the binding on the frame. Use a close stitch, oversewing the lining to the tape (5). Remove the pins as you work, and use a thimble to help you push the needle through the taut fabric and binding. When the top and bottom edges are stitched, trim away excess fabric to leave a neatly lined frame.

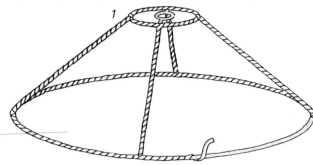

Cut two rectangles of lining fabric, considerably larger than half the shade. Lay the two rectangles, right sides facing, over one half of the shade. Pin to the struts, through both layers of fabric, stretching them tightly over the frame (2). If the frame has only three struts, cut three rectangles of lining fabric and stretch each one over the frame, right sides facing inwards, forming seams at each strut.

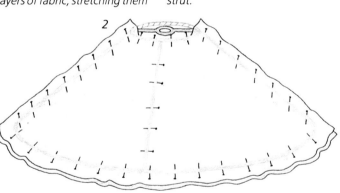

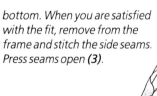

Trim away excess fabric, leaving a ½in (12mm) seam allowance down the sides where the fabric is pinned to the struts. Also leave at least 1in (2.5cm) allowance at the top and the bottom. When you are satisfied with the fit, remove from the frame and stitch the side seams. Press seams open (3).

For the pleated cover, measure the length of a strut and add 2in (5cm) for the overall depth. Measure the circumference of the bottom ring and multiply by two to give the total length of the cover (6). Join lengths if necessary on the straight grain of the fabric. Press any seams open.

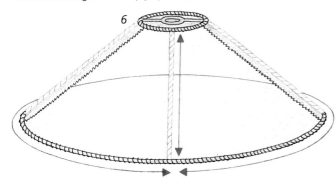

Fold under ½in (12mm) down one edge of the cover and pin it to one strut of the shade. Start to make tight pleats around the top of the shade, pinning each pleat to the top ring through the stitching holding the lining (7).

Adjust the fullness as you go; the pleats should fit neatly around the top of the frame. Arrange the final pleat to overlap the original folded edge so that you do not have to make a seam.

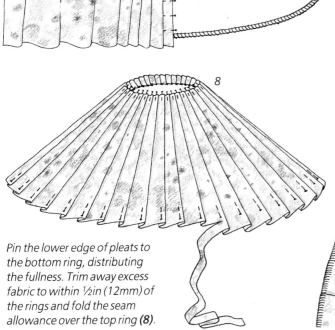

Pin the lower edge of pleats to the bottom ring, distributing the fullness. Trim away excess fabric to within ½in (12mm) of the rings and fold the seam allowance over the top ring (8).

Oversew by hand (9), removing the pins as you work. Position stitches close together and keep the fabric taut as you work. When the top of the shade is firmly stitched, stitch around the lower edge of the shade. Trim away excess fabric close to the line of stitching.

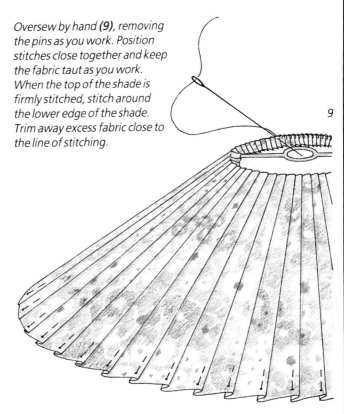

Cut a bias strip of fabric, 2in (5cm) wide, to fit around each ring. Pin one edge to pleated outside cover, right sides facing and raw edge of strip close to stitching (10). Stitch in place with a prick stitch (see page 176) ½in (12mm) from the ring. Turn in ½in (12mm) down raw edge, turn to inside and slipstitch to lining, enclosing the oversewing.

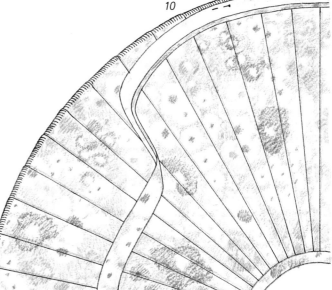

PLEATED SHADE

The selection of lampshades in the stores is often daunting and so making your own means you get exactly the colour and style you want. More often this is a problem if you want a patterned lampshade. This idea leaves the choice of pattern open. You will need a lampshade frame, strong white paper that will fold and hold a pleat, a good quality adhesive that does not stain fabric, a piece of fabric slightly larger than the paper, a leather punch and a piece of cord in a suitable colour to match the fabric on the frame.

Measure the height of the lampshade from the top ring down a strut to the bottom ring and measure the diameter straight across the centre of the bottom ring (1). Cut a piece of paper six times the length of the diameter by the height plus 2 ¼in (6cm).

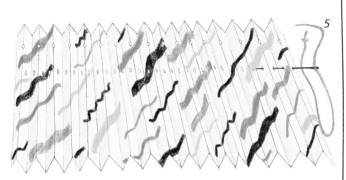

Cut out a piece of fabric the same length as the paper but 1in (2.5cm) wider. Before you cut out your fabric think about how the pattern will look on the shade. Press the fabric length and lay it right side down on a flat surface. Mark a line lightly ½in (12mm) in from both edges. Spread one side of the paper with adhesive and press onto the wrong side of the fabric, matching the marked lines along the edges (2). Fold the excess fabric over the edge of the paper and glue in place.

Working from the paper side, draw in the pleats. Using a ruler and pencil, mark horizontal lines across the width of the paper 1in (2.5cm) apart. Make sure the first line is at right angles to the edge of the paper or the pleats will not be straight (3). Fold the fabric-covered paper along each ruled line in a concertina fashion to make the pleats.

Run the back of a pair of scissors over each pleat to set it. Working from the fabric side, make the two rows of holes. The top row is a design feature and the second row has a cord threaded through it to draw up the shade to fit. Working from the fabric side and using a leather punch, make holes on the raised pleat folds 1 ½in (4cm) down from the top edge.

The next row of holes should be 4in (10cm) down from the top edges and half way along each pleat (4). Fold the pleat and make the holes through both layers of the pleat. Cut a length of cord 2in (5cm) longer than the pleated shade and thread through a long upholstery needle. Thread the cord through the second row of holes across the fabric-covered paper (5). Knot loosely at each end. Glue or staple the short edges of the shade together to form a ring. Trim the edges so that, from the right side, the raw edge is disguised inside a pleat. Place the shade over the frame and pull up the cord until it fits (6). Tie the cord in a bow.

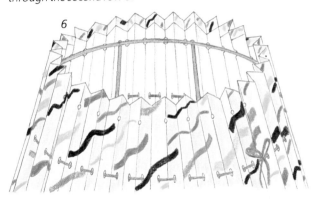

147

LINED BASKET

Lined baskets make decorative extra storage space. They are easy to carry about and ideal for storage of items such as knitting wools. Lined with a waterproof fabric, they are useful for make-up and toiletries. This design is sensible as the lip of the basket is covered by the lining thus protecting the contents from being caught on the rushwork. To line a basket with a circumference of 48in (122cm), you will need about 3 yards (2.75 metres) of a light cotton or linen.

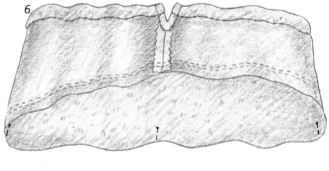

To cut the base, stand the basket on fabric and draw around it with a soft pencil (1). Cut out, adding ½in (12mm) seam allowance all around. Fold circle into quarters and mark with pins at four points on the circumference. Cut out a piece of fabric 1½ times the circumference of the top of the basket and the depth down the curve plus 3in (8cm) (1). Join short edges and press seams open (2).

Straighten fabric out with seam at one end; mark fold at opposite end to seam. Cut out a 2in (4cm) wide and 2½in (6cm) deep triangle at both points. Cut two 6½in (17cm) lengths of 1in (2.5cm) fabric cut on bias and pin along the right side of slashed openings. Machine stitch, pivoting fabric on needle to ease around the point(3). Clip fabric at the point, turn the binding, press and hem onto the wrong side (4).

Turn in ¼in (6mm) along one long edge and press. Turn in a further 1in (2.5cm), press and slipstitch along the inside edge, leaving the hem open at the bias-neatened edges (5). Fold lining in four and mark the four points at the raw edge with

pins. Run two gathering threads along the raw edge (6). Bring the bottom and lining together, wrong sides facing, matching the marked points. Ease the gathers to fit between these points. Pin, baste and machine stitch (7).

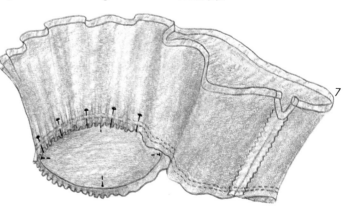

Cut a length of bias strip equal to four times the circumference of the basket top. Divide it in two and with right sides facing, stitch along raw edges. Turn out and press. Slipstitch ends closed. Thread through the casing (8).

Press and, with the wrong side down, place the lining in the basket. Turn the hemmed edge to the outside and tie the fabric ribbons so the lining is drawn up and is held firm around the basket lip.

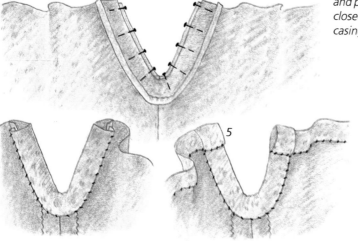

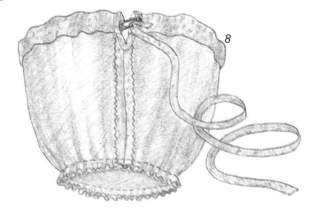

TEA COSY AND TRAY SET

The appliqué on this tea cosy, napkin and traycloth is based on a simple leaf design (see page 173). You will need ½ yard (45cm) of fabric, lining, wadding and muslin for the tea cosy, pieces of fabric for the appliqué shapes and more main fabric for the napkins and tray cloth. The appliqué shapes are finished off with embroidery stitches. Sew backstitches (see page 176) in embroidery thread for the stalk and build them up for the stamens.

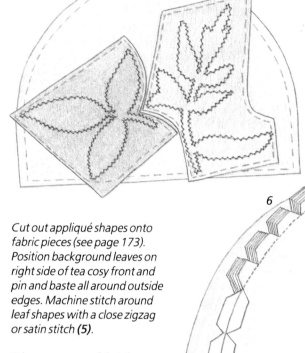

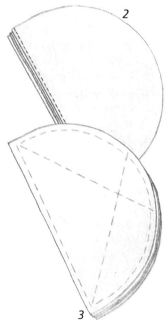

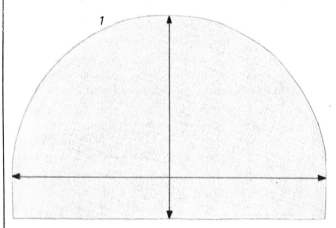

Measure the height and width of your teapot and add 1½in (4cm) to height and 2½in (6cm) to the width. A finished size of 9in (23cm) by 12in (30cm) will fit most standard teapots. Cut a paper pattern using the diagram (1) by scaling up (see page 166). Cut two pieces each of main fabric, wadding and fine muslin. Baste single layers together, fabric right side out and wadding sandwiched between the fabric and the muslin (2). Baste along outside edges and through the centre to hold (3).

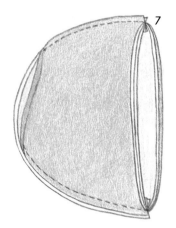

Cut out appliqué shapes onto fabric pieces (see page 173). Position background leaves on right side of tea cosy front and pin and baste all around outside edges. Machine stitch around leaf shapes with a close zigzag or satin stitch (5).

Trim away excess fabric from around the stitching line (see page 47). Pin, baste and stitch remaining shapes following the

positions in the photograph. Finish off with embroidery stitches. With right sides facing, pin and stitch two cosy sections together. Clip curves and press seams open (6).

With right sides facing(7) pin, baste and stitch lining to cover around the bottom through all layers. Turn cosy to right side through opening, slipstitch lining edges together.

Cut out two pieces of lining using the paper pattern and, right sides facing, stitch around the curved edges leaving a 4in (10cm) opening at the top (4). Press seam and opening seam allowance open.

To make traycloth and napkins see pages 104-107. Omit final hem stitching. Instead place appliqué motifs close to the edges on right side of napkin. Stitch appliqué as before and trim away excess fabric, including bottom corner of napkin (8). Topstitch hems on all sides with a double layer of satin stitch.

IDEAS FOR FINISHING TOUCHES

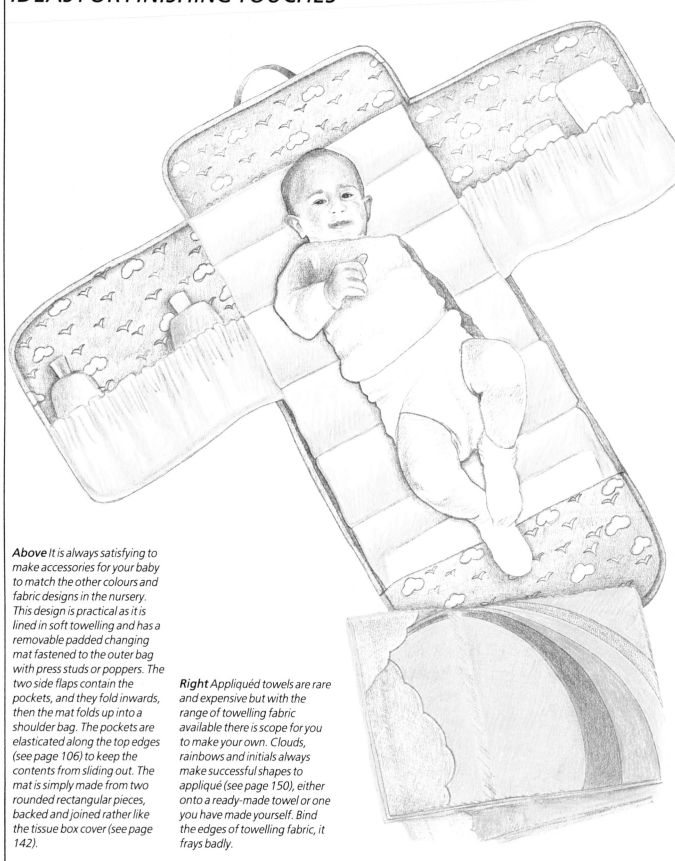

Above It is always satisfying to make accessories for your baby to match the other colours and fabric designs in the nursery. This design is practical as it is lined in soft towelling and has a removable padded changing mat fastened to the outer bag with press studs or poppers. The two side flaps contain the pockets, and they fold inwards, then the mat folds up into a shoulder bag. The pockets are elasticated along the top edges (see page 106) to keep the contents from sliding out. The mat is simply made from two rounded rectangular pieces, backed and joined rather like the tissue box cover (see page 142).

Right Appliquéd towels are rare and expensive but with the range of towelling fabric available there is scope for you to make your own. Clouds, rainbows and initials always make successful shapes to appliqué (see page 150), either onto a ready-made towel or one you have made yourself. Bind the edges of towelling fabric, it frays badly.

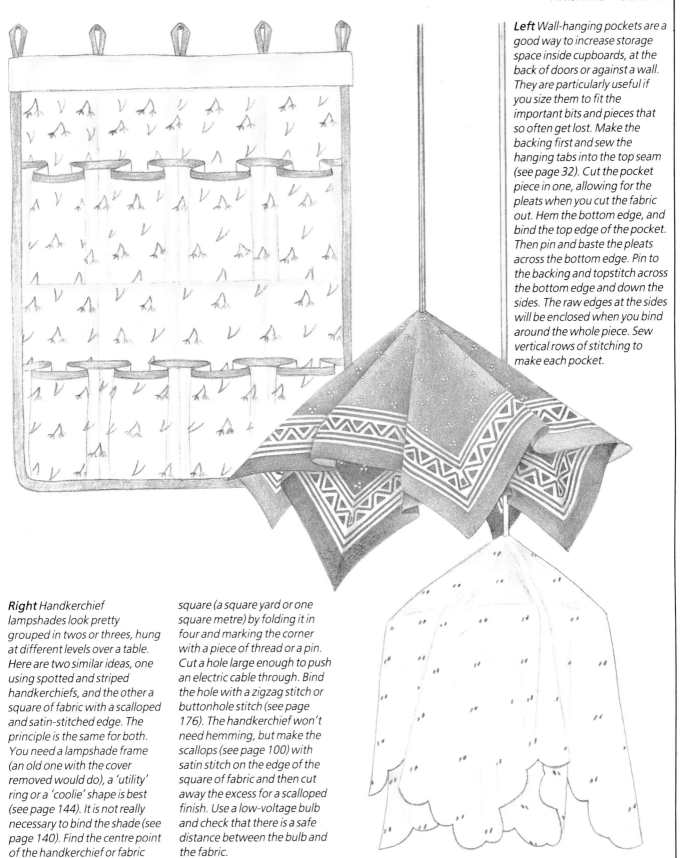

Left Wall-hanging pockets are a good way to increase storage space inside cupboards, at the back of doors or against a wall. They are particularly useful if you size them to fit the important bits and pieces that so often get lost. Make the backing first and sew the hanging tabs into the top seam (see page 32). Cut the pocket piece in one, allowing for the pleats when you cut the fabric out. Hem the bottom edge, and bind the top edge of the pocket. Then pin and baste the pleats across the bottom edge. Pin to the backing and topstitch across the bottom edge and down the sides. The raw edges at the sides will be enclosed when you bind around the whole piece. Sew vertical rows of stitching to make each pocket.

Right Handkerchief lampshades look pretty grouped in twos or threes, hung at different levels over a table. Here are two similar ideas, one using spotted and striped handkerchiefs, and the other a square of fabric with a scalloped and satin-stitched edge. The principle is the same for both. You need a lampshade frame (an old one with the cover removed would do), a 'utility' ring or a 'coolie' shape is best (see page 144). It is not really necessary to bind the shade (see page 140). Find the centre point of the handkerchief or fabric square (a square yard or one square metre) by folding it in four and marking the corner with a piece of thread or a pin. Cut a hole large enough to push an electric cable through. Bind the hole with a zigzag stitch or buttonhole stitch (see page 176). The handkerchief won't need hemming, but make the scallops (see page 100) with satin stitch on the edge of the square of fabric and then cut away the excess for a scalloped finish. Use a low-voltage bulb and check that there is a safe distance between the bulb and the fabric.

153

THE GREAT OUTDOORS

When your deck chair wears out, the job of replacing the covers is far easier to tackle than you might think. There are many other outdoor items, such as picnic rugs, beach bags and wind breaks, which are satisfying to make yourself. Obviously you need to choose fabrics carefully, but you will find there is a wide range of punchy, striped canvas and PVC prints to choose from. Make sure your sewing machine can stand the strain of thick canvas, and use thick threads and larger needles.

F or outdoor dining, these roll-up mats hold all the necessary cutlery and table napkins. For four napkins, you will need 1 yard (1 metre) each of the two contrasting fabrics and washable, iron-on interfacing, and 10 1/2 yards (10 metres) of a contrasting 1in (2.5cm) wide binding.

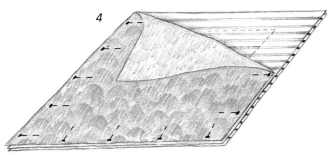

4

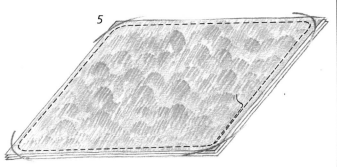

5

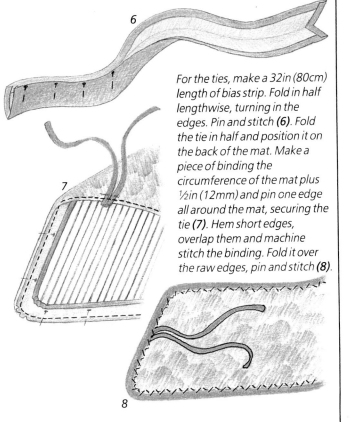

1

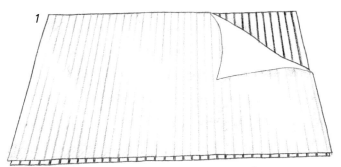

For each mat, cut one piece 12 × 18in (30 × 46cm) from both fabrics and interfacing. Position interfacing on the wrong side of the uppermost fabric piece and iron it in place (1). For the pocket, cut out two pieces of striped fabric each 7 × 9in (18 × 23cm). Place the pieces right sides facing, pin and stitch together, leaving a central opening on one side. Trim and clip across the corners. Turn to the right side and slipstitch opening (2). For the napkin holder, cut two pieces 3 × 4in (8 × 10cm) and make in the same way as the pocket.

2

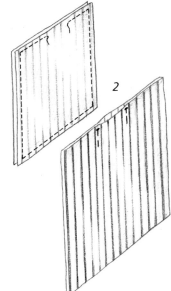

Pin the piece of backing fabric to the top section, wrong sides facing (4). Stitch all around the mat, keeping the stitching ¼in (6mm) in from the outside edge. Using a round plate, round off the corners and cut along the marked lines (5).

6

For the ties, make a 32in (80cm) length of bias strip. Fold in half lengthwise, turning in the edges. Pin and stitch (6). Fold the tie in half and position it on the back of the mat. Make a piece of binding the circumference of the mat plus ½in (12mm) and pin one edge all around the mat, securing the tie (7). Hem short edges, overlap them and machine stitch the binding. Fold it over the raw edges, pin and stitch (8).

3

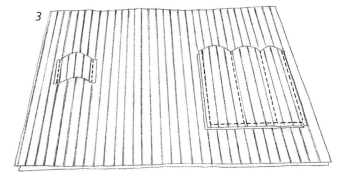

7

Centre the pocket 1½in (4cm) in from the right-hand edge. Pin and topstitch the sides and the bottom edge. Divide the pocket into three equal sections, pin

and topstitch down the dividing lines. Centre the napkin holder 1½in (4cm) in from the left side. Pin and topstitch in place (3).

8

DAISY PICNIC MAT

This giant daisy makes an original and eye-catching picnic mat. The design is appealing because of its practicality and for the sheer fun of each picnic guest being allocated a separate petal to eat off. Each petal is a pocket in which to slot a plate or cutlery. To save the fuss of laying the place settings when you reach the picnic spot, the whole daisy can be pre-packed and folded with unbreakable plates and cutlery inside, and then carefully unfolded when you arrive.

You could either make up the design from lightweight waterproof canvas, or use a vinyl fabric for the backing and a lighter, densely woven cotton material for the pockets. Alternatively, you could make the entire design out of wipeable PVC, and if you have young, messy eaters in the family, this could be the sensible solution. However, what you gain in practical terms with the vinyl fabric has to be weighed against its disadvantages. It is difficult to feed through a sewing machine because the waterproof glossy side tends to stick under the sewing machine foot. One way around this problem is to dust the surface lightly with talcum powder, or to cover the shiny side with a piece of tissue paper which can be torn away when the seam has been sewn.

To make up this design you will need 1½ yards (1.4 metres) of the coloured fabric, in a reversible woven cotton; a generous ½ yard (45cm) of the contrasting fabric; and 6 yards (5.5 metres) of bias binding.

Make up a paper pattern for the egg-shaped petal **(1)** and then cut out eight complete petals, adding a ½in (12mm) seam allowance all around. Cut out eight half petals adding ½in (12mm) allowance around the curved sides and 1in (2.5cm)

along the straight edge. Cut two centre circles using a dinner plate with a diameter of 12in (30cm). You can make a circular pattern following the method for cutting a circular tablecloth shown on page 106.

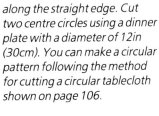

Turn under ½in (12mm) seam allowance all around a circle piece, clipping into the seam allowance to make a flat edge **(5)**. Lay the circle piece, wrong side uppermost, on a large, flat

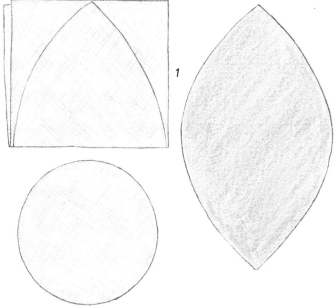

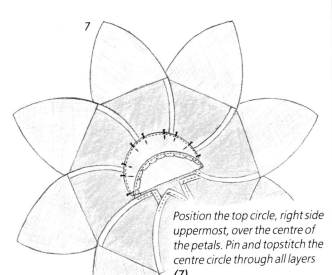

Turn under ¼in (6mm) and then ¾in (2cm) along the straight edge of the half petal; pin and stitch **(2)**. Place one half petal on a complete petal, right

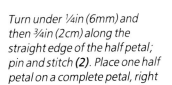

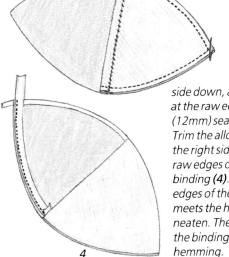

surface. Position the petals onto it, overlapping them slightly each time on the left-hand edge. Pin and stitch the petals in position through all layers when

you have the desired effect **(6)**. Prepare the other circle piece and baste the hem to hold it in place.

side down, and stitch together at the raw edges, taking a ½in (12mm) seam allowance **(3)**. Trim the allowance and turn to the right side. Press. Bind the raw edges of the petal with bias binding **(4)**. Fold under the raw edges of the binding where it meets the half petal and hem to neaten. The overlapping ends of the binding do not need hemming.

Position the top circle, right side uppermost, over the centre of the petals. Pin and topstitch the centre circle through all layers **(7)**.

DECK CHAIR

A pillow decorated with simple appliqué motifs (see page 166) makes this deck chair individual and more comfortable. A finishing touch would be to paint the chair in a colour that blends with the new cover. You will need a sturdy fabric such as canvas for the cover and pillow, wadding or a tiny cushion pad, fabric pieces for the appliqué shapes, 60in (155cm) of ribbon to tie the pillow to the frame of the chair and tacks to attach the cover to the frame.

To measure the deck chair for a replacement cover, lay the collapsed chair face down and place a tape measure along the length of the seat frame, carrying the tape around the full depth of the end struts. The fabric should cover the struts on all sides with a 1in (2.5cm) hem allowed at either end (1). If the original cover is intact, remove it and use for a pattern. Lift out all old tacks with a claw hammer and tap any that cannot be removed flush with the wooden frame. Fill holes and sand the surface smooth.

To prepare new cover, cut out fabric and fold 1in (2.5cm) hems at both short ends. Press. Hem long edges, if necessary; turn under ¼in (6mm) and zigzag stitch over raw edge. Lay fabric right side down on the floor and lay the deck chair face down on top. Bring fabric around one end of frame and butt hemmed edge up close to the underside of the strut. Anchor it in place at the centre point with a tack and, working outwards, evenly space tacks to edges (2). Turn chair around, pull fabric taut and tack other end in position. Cut two pieces of fabric for the cushion cover the width of the chair and 10in (25cm) deep, allowing ½in (12mm) all around.

Trace appliqué motifs onto fabric with a soft pencil (see page 166) and iron on interfacing. Lay fabric with motifs on them onto one cushion piece, pin and baste in place. Using matching thread, zigzag stitch along design lines (3). Stitch internal lines as well. With sharp scissors, cut away excess fabric from around motifs close to stitching.

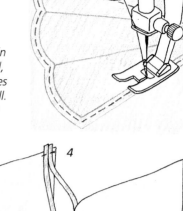

Cut a 60 in (155cm) length of ribbon into four pieces and pin two pieces at each corner on the top cushion cover (4). With right sides facing, pin, baste and machine stitch cushion cover, leaving an 8in (20cm) opening along the top edge.

Stuff cover loosely with desired filling (see page 182), turn in raw edges, pin and slipstitch closed (5). Attach cushion to chair frame and tie at front (6).

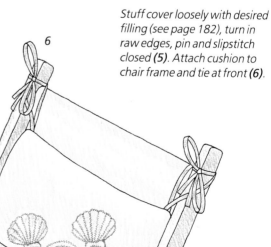

DIRECTOR'S CHAIR

Repairing garden furniture is tremendously rewarding because the results are so quick and transforming. Often the removal of the old covers – getting out the old tacks and making good – takes longer than the creative job of making a new cover. For this chair a canvas replacement is a sensible choice, like this bright primary stripe. Although it is possible to use a tightly woven linen or even nylon canvas, don't expect your covers to last as long as the canvas will. You will need about 1 yard (1 metre) of your chosen fabric, all-purpose filler and wide-headed tacks. For indoor use, you could make a more sophisticated cover for a director's chair. Old oriental carpet pieces neatened up and bound along the edges make unusual covers. A large floral, backed with a tough lining, can look quite stunning, particularly if you paint the frame a bright colour.

To prepare the director's chair for re-covering, remove the old cover carefully. Slide backrest off uprights *(1)*, unpick casings, open out folds and press. Use as a pattern to cut the new backrest. If you have no old cover, measure the distance

between the two uprights and add 12in (30cm) for the two casings. Turn under ½in (12mm) to wrong side of both long edges and press. Turn in a further ½in (12mm) and topstitch close to hemmed edge. Turn in ½in (12mm) along both short edges and then make a further turning for the casings. Pin and check for fit. Topstitch casings.

Remove hinges from either side of seat and set armrests aside *(2)*. Pull seat fabric away from fixing tacks and remove loose tacks with pliers. Ease tacks out gently, taking care not to split the frame, and fill holes with all-purpose filler. Tap any stubborn tacks back into the wood, flush with the surface *(3)*. Open out folds of fabric, press and use as a pattern for new seat.

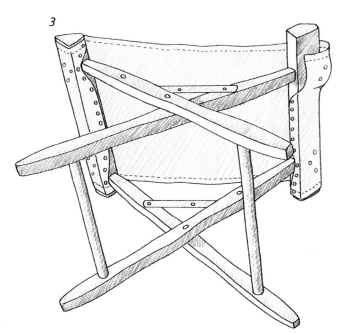

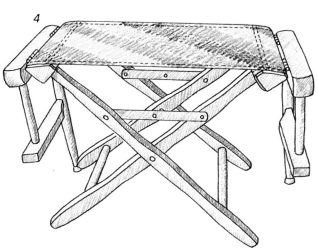

If you haven't an old cover, measure across the width of the open chair from the outside edges. Add ample turning allowance to give a double thickness of fabric on the other two sides of the rail. To make up the seat, hem long edges with a double ½in (12mm) hem. Turn ½in (12mm) to wrong side of short edges and press. Turn in remaining allowance to give a deep double hem and topstitch close to edges.

Invert chair onto a flat surface and lay one folded edge of fabric to the underside of one seat rail. Keeping fabric taut, tack in position at centre and both outside edges and space remaining tacks in between, shaping fabric around chair leg.

Stretch fabric across to opposite seat rail and tack in position as before *(4)*. Take care to avoid remaining tack heads. Mark positions of screw holes for hinges and replace armrests by screwing hinges back in place. Slot backrest over uprights.

IDEAS FOR OUTDOORS

With such a wide range of hardy and waterproof fabrics available, it is fun to make or adapt your own designs for picnics and the seaside. A large beach umbrella can double up as a windbreak too. Choose a light fabric and attach it to the umbrella either with large press studs or sew loops to the edges of the umbrella and ties to the windbreak. Make loops along the bottom edge too so the fabric can be skewered into the ground like a tent.

If you are re-covering a deck chair, make a padded towelling cover for extra comfort. Make the canvas cover (see page 160), but before applying it to the frame, lie wadding over it and then towelling or use a large beach towel. Hem the edges and topstitch them to the canvas base. Machine stitch along the stripes to give a quilted effect.

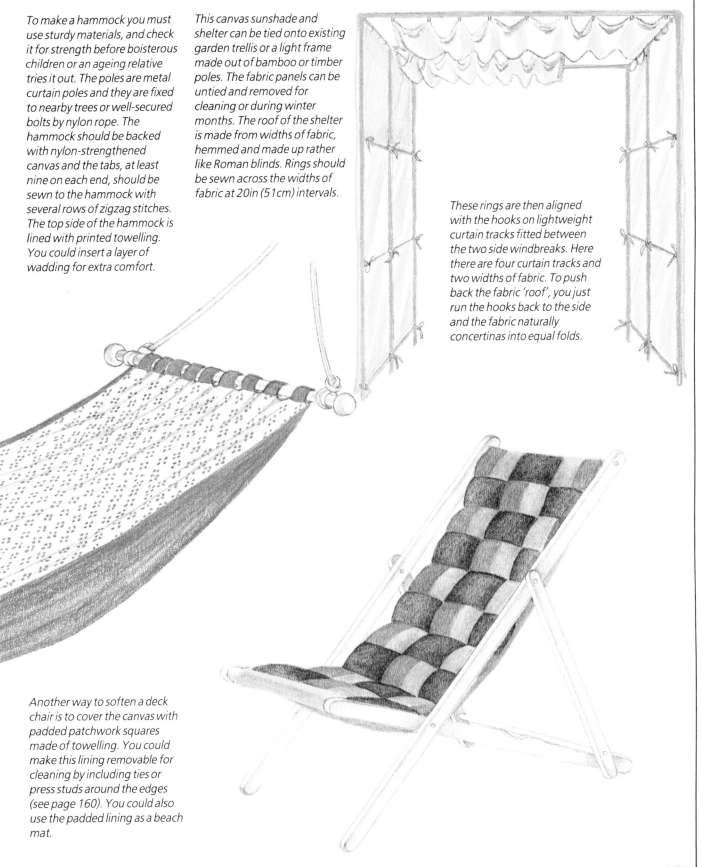

To make a hammock you must use sturdy materials, and check it for strength before boisterous children or an ageing relative tries it out. The poles are metal curtain poles and they are fixed to nearby trees or well-secured bolts by nylon rope. The hammock should be backed with nylon-strengthened canvas and the tabs, at least nine on each end, should be sewn to the hammock with several rows of zigzag stitches. The top side of the hammock is lined with printed towelling. You could insert a layer of wadding for extra comfort.

This canvas sunshade and shelter can be tied onto existing garden trellis or a light frame made out of bamboo or timber poles. The fabric panels can be untied and removed for cleaning or during winter months. The roof of the shelter is made from widths of fabric, hemmed and made up rather like Roman blinds. Rings should be sewn across the widths of fabric at 20in (51cm) intervals.

These rings are then aligned with the hooks on lightweight curtain tracks fitted between the two side windbreaks. Here there are four curtain tracks and two widths of fabric. To push back the fabric 'roof', you just run the hooks back to the side and the fabric naturally concertinas into equal folds.

Another way to soften a deck chair is to cover the canvas with padded patchwork squares made of towelling. You could make this lining removable for cleaning by including ties or press studs around the edges (see page 160). You could also use the padded lining as a beach mat.

MOTIFS AND STENCILS

An effective way to decorate fabric is to appliqué shapes onto it or paint a design using a stencil. Reproduced on the following pages you will find the motifs and stencils which appear in this book. To copy the shape, simply trace around it using tracing paper and a felt-tip pen. If the design is too big or too small for your purposes, there are two easy ways to change the scale. Either take your tracing to a photocopier's and they will make copies to a larger or smaller format; or trace the pattern onto a piece of graph paper, and following the intersections of the graph, redraw the pattern onto graph paper with a larger or smaller grid. You then cut out the pattern and transfer it to the fabric. Pencil around the shape, drawing straight onto the fabric. The pencil lines will be covered by the machined satin stitch. If you prefer to work from the wrong side, straight stitch around the pencilled design from the wrong side. The stitches will show on the right side. This is the way to transfer internal design lines too. It is a good idea to back your appliqué work with iron-on interfacing. The excess is cut away with the fabric when all the sewing is completed. Use sharp, small embroidery scissors for this job.

To cut the stencil, simply trace the pattern onto a piece of stiff card or, if you are repeating the design often, onto clear plastic. Cut the shapes out with a special craft knife for a clean cut.

Appliquéd roller blind (page 48) and deck chair (page 160)
These shell shapes are applied along the bottom edge and at random on the roller blind. They are reproduced here to a size suitable for an average window. These shapes are also used on the pillow attached to the deck chair. The double lines around the shapes represent the approximate width of the machine zigzag or satin stitch.

Appliquéd kitchen curtain (page 62)
The flower and clover leaf design opposite is made up using two different coloured fabrics; red for the flower and green for the leaves. The stalks are made by machine stitching only. The motif is drawn on a graph so that it can easily be enlarged or reduced.

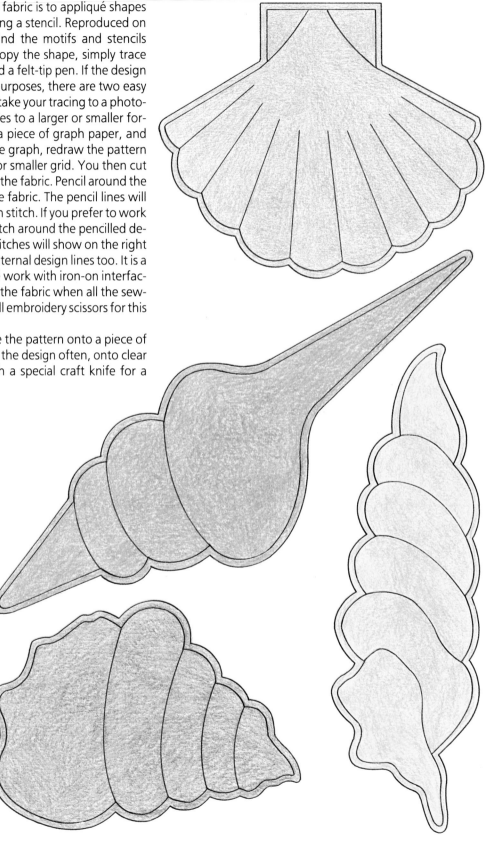

Quilted cushions (page 92)

Most of the patterns on these quilted cushions are made with straight lines. You will need a ruler and a pencil; a set square would also be useful. If you use the ready-quilted nylon wadding you will have a grid of lines which will help you to build up the pattern evenly. You could trace this pattern onto a sheet of graph paper the same size as the illustrations here and transpose the lines onto the nylon wadding. The colour of these illustrations relates to the cushion colour in the photograph.

Appliquéd cushions (page 98)
These shapes represent the flowers in the appliqué. To make the leaves, trace off one of the petals and apply as shown in the photograph.

Cloth with pumpkin appliqué (page 108)
Decide on the size of your motif. Take a sheet of paper and mark a rectangle to indicate the outer limits of the pumpkin with its stalks and leaves. Divide the rectangle up into the same number of equal-sized squares as there are on this grid over the pumpkin motif. Take each square separately and enlarge the lines in that square to fit your larger or smaller squares. Cut paper patterns for each section of the motif, adding ½in (12mm) seam allowance all around.

Patchwork quilt (page 130)
Cut the templates for the quilt directly from these shapes. The border around the shapes represents the seam allowance. Cut the template out of stiff card so that it can be re-used. Cut a few templates as constant cutting will wear away the edges and make them inaccurate. The square you can make yourself; it is 1in (2.5cm) square, plus ¼in (6mm) allowance all around.

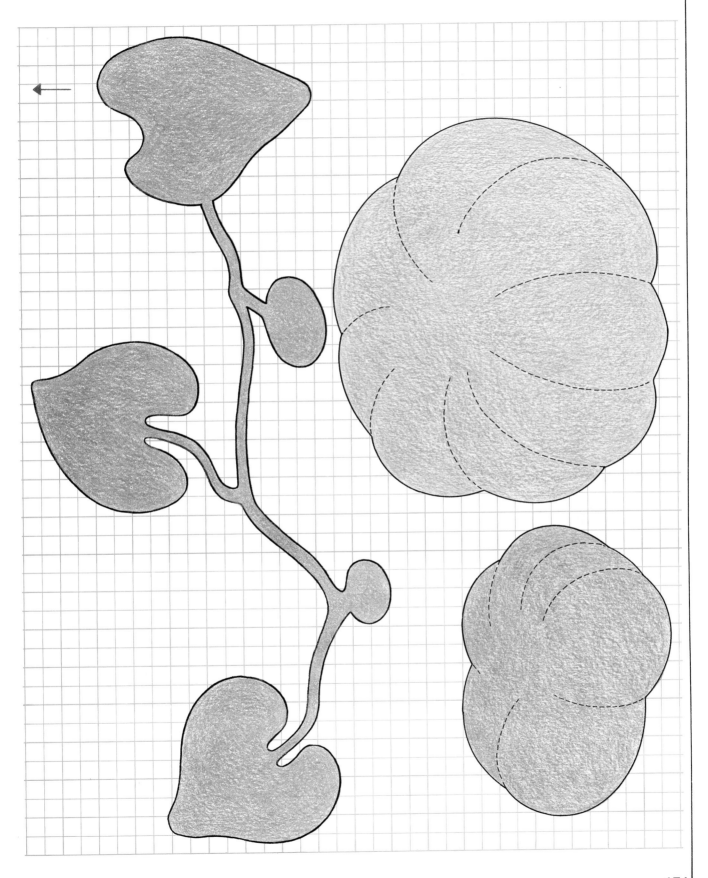

Stencilled bedspread (page 126)

Trace and cut out your stencil and try out the colours on a piece of paper first. The arrow on this diagram indicates the top of the design and should be placed towards the head and the foot of the bed. The other

repeats of the stencil are then spaced in between. This stencil has been cut to a size which would be suitable for a bedspread on a double bed. If you need to scale it down for a single bed or a child's cot delete some outer leaves, or use fewer repeats. Note that the space between each hole is sufficient to prevent the paint from running.

Tea cosy and napkins (page 150)
These shapes are built up into a busy design on the tea cosy, but on the tray cloth and the napkins they have been used singly on the edges. Cut out the shapes first and experiment with them. You may come up with a different combination to the one shown. The internal design lines are made with machine stitching and embroidery stitches.

SEWING TECHNIQUES

Like any other skill, sewing is easy once the basic know-how becomes second nature. Here is a quick and easy guide to show or remind you how to do the basic stitches. You will also find here some of the easy tricks of the trade, which make all the difference between an average and a professional finish. Finally, there is a guide to fabrics, and how to look after them.

STITCHES AND SEAMS

Stitches

Handsewing is usually the final step in the completion of a project. It has to be neat and it does take time, but working directly on the fabric means that you have more control than with a sewing machine.

1 Basting
2 Gathering
3 Backstitch
4 Slipstitch
5 Hemming
6 Prickstitch
7 Oversewing
8 Blanket stitch
9 Buttonhole
10 Herringbone
11 Lockstitch

1 Basting This is simply a line of large running stitches. Begin with a knot and take large, even stitches along the seam line.

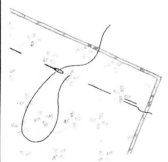

2 Gathering Begin with a backstitch **(3)** and work two rows of running stitches ⅛in (3mm) apart on either side of seam line. Pull up together and wind around a pin to hold.

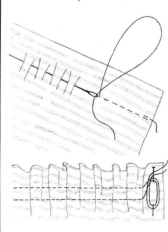

3 Backstitch This is the hand-sewn equivalent of a machine stitch. Work from right to left making small even stitches.

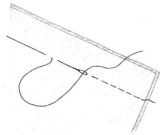

4 Slipstitch Take a small stitch inside the fold and then catch some threads on the piece of fabric to be joined opposite your first stitch.

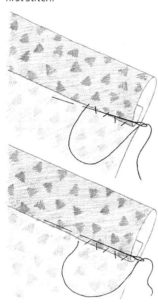

5 Hemming Work small slanting stitches through the fabric and the hem. Stitches must be small and even as they show through on the right side.

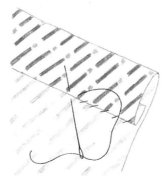

6 Prickstitch Similar to backstitch **(3)** but this is worked from the right side and only a couple of threads are picked up with each stitch.

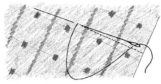

7 Oversewing Work slanting stitches about ⅛in (3mm) long over the raw edge. They should be level with the edge and not be pulled tight.

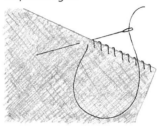

8 Blanket stitch Put the needle through fabric ¼in (6mm) from fabric edge. Hold the thread under needle point and pull the needle through, forming a loop.

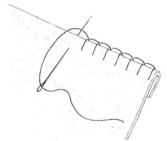

9 Buttonhole stitch Work in the opposite direction to blanket stitch **(8)**. Take the thread and twist it round the needle point. Pull the needle through, forming a knot on the raw edge of the fabric.

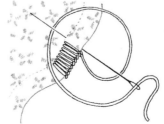

10 Herringbone stitch Working from left to right, take a short horizontal stitch with the needle pointing from right to left. Take another stitch on the piece of fabric to be joined. Do not pull tight.

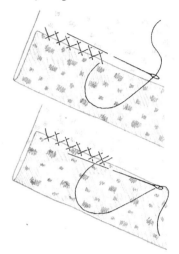

11 Lockstitch This is worked like blanket stitch **(8)** but very loosely. Place the main fabric flat on a surface. Pin the second piece of fabric, which is the lining, wrong sides facing, on top. Fold back the second piece of fabric in a straight line and

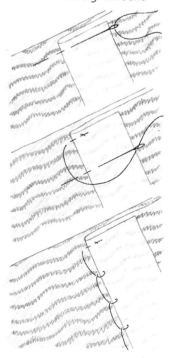

work the stitches through the fold of the lining fabric and into the flat curtain fabric. Pick up only a single thread at a time. To ensure that the two layers of fabric hang loosely and do not pull against one another, do not pull the stitches too tight. Make the stitches at intervals of about 2in (5cm) along the line of your work.

Seams
1 Flat fell seam
2 Topstitched seam
3 French seam
4 Mock French seam
5 Lapped seam

1 Flat fell seam *With right sides of fabric facing, pin and stitch seam leaving a ½in (12mm) allowance. Trim one allowance down to ¼in (6mm). Fold wider allowance in half, enclosing other allowance and press flat. Pin and stitch along folded edge.*

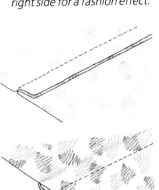

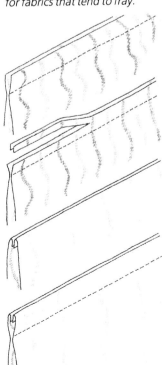

2 Topstitched seam *Pin and stitch seam with right sides facing, taking a ½in (12mm) seam allowance. Press both allowances to one side. Pin and stitch through all layers from the right side for a fashion effect.*

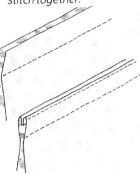

3 French seam *Pin and stitch a ¼in (6mm) seam with wrong sides facing. Trim any frayed edges and press seam closed with right sides facing along the seam line. Pin and stitch seam again ½in (12mm) from the folded edge, enclosing the raw edges as you sew. This is ideal for fabrics that tend to fray.*

4 Mock French seam *Pin and stitch seam, right sides facing, with a ½in (12mm) seam allowance. Fold both allowances in half towards the inside of the seam. Pin and stitch together.*

5 Lapped seam *Turn under one edge of fabric for ¼in (6mm) and place it to the right side of a second piece of fabric ½in (12mm) from the raw edge. Pin and machine stitch along the*

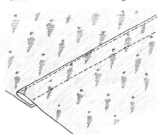

fold, working from the right side of the fabric. Pin and stitch again enclosing the raw edges.

Seam finishes
1 Pinking
2 Zigzag stitching
3 Edgestitched seams
4 Self-bound seams
5 Bias binding

1 Pinking *Simply cut along the seam allowances using pinking shears.*

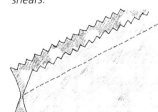

2 Zigzag stitching *Adjust the stitch size according to fabric and zigzag along the raw edges on a swing-needle machine.*

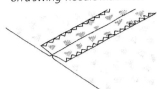

3 Edgestitched seams *Press seam open and turn under ⅛in (3mm) along both raw edges. Pin and stitch hems close to fold.*

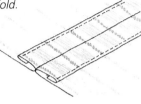

4 Self-bound seams *With right sides facing, pin and stitch the seam with a ½in (12mm) allowance. Trim one allowance to half its width and fold the other allowance over it. Turn under and slipstitch along line of seam.*

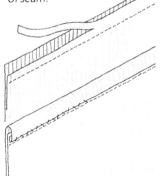

5 Bias binding *Fold bias binding lengthwise and place over raw edges of the seam allowances. Pin and stitch in place, keeping within the seam allowance.*

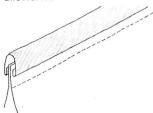

SEWING TECHNIQUES

1 Bias binding *To find the bias grain, fold the selvedge so that it lies parallel to the weft. Cut along the fold and use this edge for cutting bias strips. Join the strips together on the straight grain.*

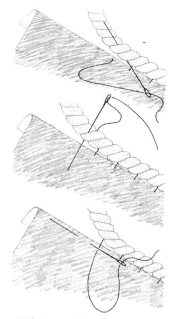

2 Cord trim *To apply cord in a straight line, simply place it along the seam line, after tucking the end to the wrong side. Stitch through cord and fabric with small stitches.*

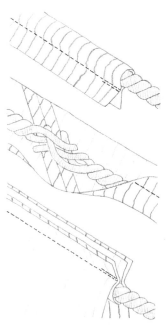

3 Piping *Fold binding around cord and stitch close to cord. To join ends, sew fabric strips together, unravel 1in (2.5cm) of cord and trim strands to stagger lengths. Twist them around each other.*

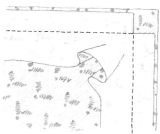

4 Corners *After stitching, trim straight across fabric at corner close to stitches.*

5 Sharp corners *Work one or two stitches across the corner. The number of stitches will depend on the fabric thickness. Trim the fabric as shown.*

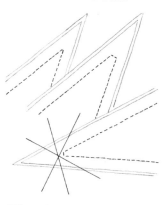

6 Boxed corner *Stitch up to the corner. Cut a small square of fabric at the corner point. Continue to stitch down the other side. Reinforce corner.*

7 Curves *After stitching an inside or outside curve, clip notches into the seam allowance.*

8 Bound edge *Turn under ¼in (6mm) hem along one side, press. Stitch binding to fabric, right sides facing, fold over to wrong side and stitch.*

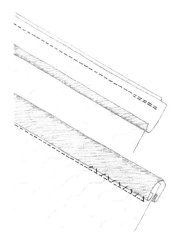

9 Mitred edges *Stitch trimming to corner point and mark corner across trimming. Sew trimming pieces together with right sides facing along marked lines. Trim seam allowance and press corner open. Turn under raw edges and sew to main fabric.*

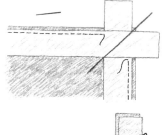

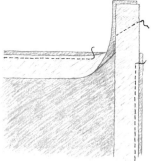

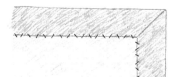

10 Mitred corners Make a ¼in (6mm) hem and then another 1in (2.5cm) hem and press. Open out the 1in (2.5cm) hem. Make a fold across the corner so that the fold line is ¼in (6mm) from the intersection of the two original fold lines. Cut across the corner on this new fold line and turn in ¼in (6mm). Refold the hem and slipstitch the folded edges together at the corner. Then finish off the other hems.

11 Ruffles Divide ruffle and item to be ruffled into equal sections. Gather each ruffled section in turn and pull up to fit. Pin and stitch in place.

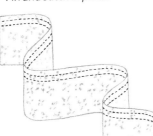

13 Matching patterns Press under seam allowance on one fabric piece and place to right side of second piece. Stitch from right side as shown.

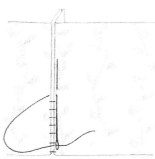

16 Zips It is usually best to insert the zip at the beginning of the work. To centre a zip, baste a flat seam, press open and pin and baste the zip in place with the teeth centred over the seam. Stitch, and unpick the basted seam.

An invisible zip is inserted with a special zip foot. The stitching line is close to the teeth of the zip. From the right side only the zip tab is seen. To overlap a zip, press the seam allowance in one

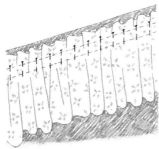

14 Sheer fabrics When working with difficult fabrics, place a layer of tissue between the two pieces to be sewn. Tear away after stitching the seam.

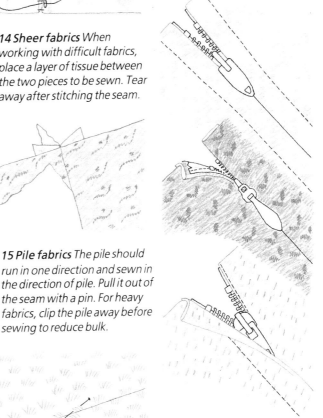

12 Self-bound ruffle Trim away excess seam allowance from the ruffle. Fold the fabric allowance over, turning under a small hem, and slipstitch along seam line.

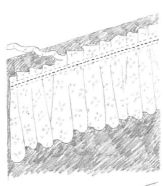

15 Pile fabrics The pile should run in one direction and sewn in the direction of pile. Pull it out of the seam with a pin. For heavy fabrics, clip the pile away before sewing to reduce bulk.

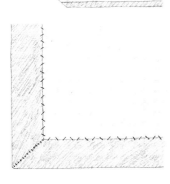

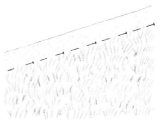

direction, and then turn back one side leaving a ¼in (6mm) overlap at the seam. Pin and tack the zip with the teeth close to this narrower allowance. Overlap the other side to hide the zip and pin and baste. Machine stitch zip in place and stitch across the foot of the zip.

MEASURING UP

Measuring up for your window dressing or bedspread is not just a matter of calculating the amount of fabric required and making the cutting plan. It also involves deciding upon the sort of effect you want; whether you want the windows to appear larger or smaller or whether the bed is to have a tailored valance or a luxurious ruffled look.

When measuring the window it is important to put up the curtain track or pole first so you know the width and height of the curtains. Then decide on the heading tape – this will also affect your calculations. Your measurements should be taken of the actual area the curtain is to cover. The illustrations here give the hanging positions:

1 Floor-to-ceiling curtains
2 Café curtains
3 Roller blind or curtains inside the window recess
4 Wall-fixed curtains
Multiply the width of the window by the width needed for your particular heading tape: 1½-2 times for standard gathering tape; 2¼-2½ for pencil pleating; 2-2½ for pinch pleats. These figures will vary according to your needs. Check the figure the manufacturer recommends if you're not sure. It is always better to be generous, however. Add allowances for the heading and the hem; this too will vary. Heavy curtains need larger hems and sheer curtains may have a rolled hem of only ¼in (6mm).

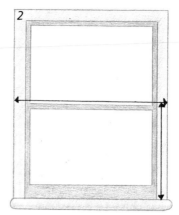

Also you must decide whether the top of the curtain is to be flush with the top of the curtain track or raised above it. This will depend on which row you thread the hanging hooks from. Lastly, add allowances for the side hems, and if the curtains overlap when drawn, add 4-6in (10-15cm).

If you have chosen a patterned fabric, then you must make allowances for the pattern repeats. For example, each length will have a certain number of pattern repeats. Even if the length is 42in (106cm) and the pattern repeat every 10in (25cm), you will need five repeats, or 50in (127cm) for every length. Also plan where the focal point of your pattern is to be. For floor-length curtains, attention is drawn to the top part, so make sure your pattern is well displayed there. On sill-length curtains, the lower edge is more noticeable, so end the repeat neatly at the hem.

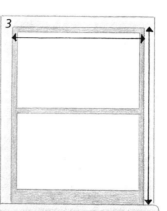

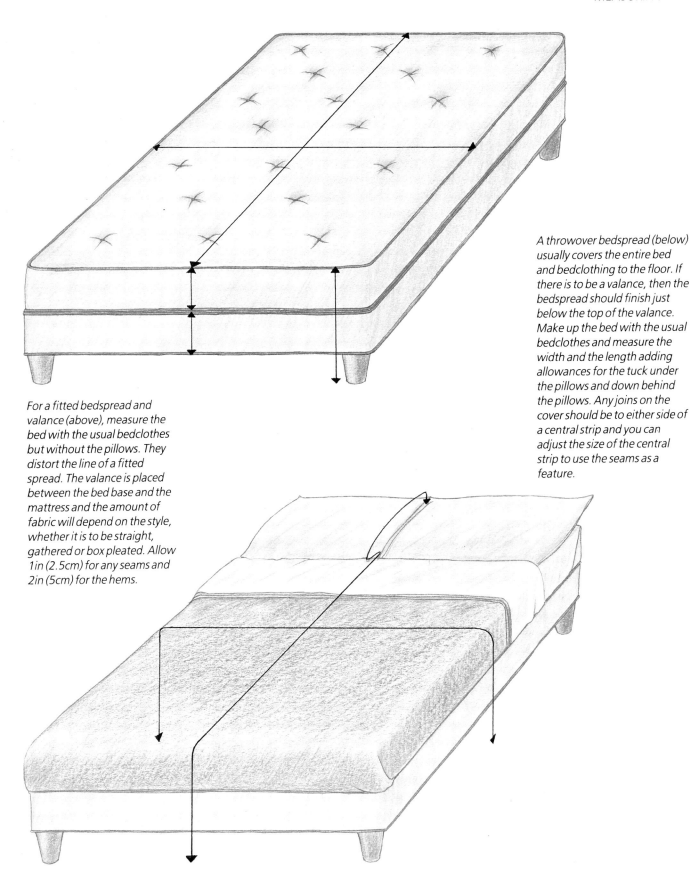

A throverover bedspread (below) usually covers the entire bed and bedclothing to the floor. If there is to be a valance, then the bedspread should finish just below the top of the valance. Make up the bed with the usual bedclothes and measure the width and the length adding allowances for the tuck under the pillows and down behind the pillows. Any joins on the cover should be to either side of a central strip and you can adjust the size of the central strip to use the seams as a feature.

For a fitted bedspread and valance (above), measure the bed with the usual bedclothes but without the pillows. They distort the line of a fitted spread. The valance is placed between the bed base and the mattress and the amount of fabric will depend on the style, whether it is to be straight, gathered or box pleated. Allow 1in (2.5cm) for any seams and 2in (5cm) for the hems.

FABRIC CARE

If you have taken a lot of trouble to make something for your home, it is worth caring for it so that it lasts and keeps its looks. Find out about the fabric you are using. If the fabric is washable, test a square for shrinkage, and if it shrinks wash the entire length before you cut it out. The safe solution is to have everything dry cleaned.

Light not only fades fabric colours but it can damage the fibres too. Line curtains in sunny rooms and don't put sofas or chairs too near a window. Keep them clean; they last better if they are cleaned at least once a year. Lampshades should be dusted regularly with a feather duster or suction cleaner and if you have a specific stain, refer to the check list opposite. Here are some general tips for stain removal.

Speed is vital. Old stains are far more difficult to remove. Mop up as much as possible right away with tissue or a paper towel. Pour salt over highly coloured liquid stains such as red wine, fruit juice and blood. This absorbs the moisture and some of the colour. When attacking a stain, work from the outer edge towards the middle. This stops the stain from spreading any further. If you are applying a solvent to the stain, lay a piece of blotting paper, clean cloth or tissue beneath it to absorb the dirt. Otherwise you will simply distribute the dirt around the fabric. Dab a stain, do not rub. Rubbing also spreads the mark. When dealing with persistent stains, work from the underside of the fabric, pushing the stain up to the surface.

If the fabric is washable, soak non-greasy stains in cold water. If you can't soak, then sponge them. If the fabric is particularly valuable and you are in any doubt as to what to do, consult a professional dry cleaner.

To test for colour fastness, find a patch that will not show (a tuck in the hem or a piece from a wide seam), and test it first. Apply the stain remover, then lay your patch on a clean white piece of cloth, sandwich it with another piece and press with a warm iron. If the colour shows on the white cloth, take the fabric to a cleaner's and don't attempt a remedy yourself.

Stain removers to keep in stock

There are certain substances that are useful for stain removal and can be kept in small quantities in clearly marked containers and out of the reach of children as they are all highly toxic.

Ammonia should be used in a diluted form – 1 part ammonia to 3 parts water is usual.

Amyl acetate is like a nail varnish remover but is safe on acetate fabrics. It is flammable and should be used with care.

Biological detergent is designed to act on protein-based stains such as blood, milk and eggs. Soak the fabric overnight (except for wool, silk or any fabric with a special finish).

Bleach is good for stains on white cotton or linen. Always dilute well with water and soak the whole item. Rinse thoroughly. (Do not soak silk, wool or special finishes.)

Borax comes in a powered form. Dilute it with water, about 2 teaspoons to 1 pint (560ml) warm water.

Glycerine is good for softening old stains, thus making them easier to treat.

Hydrogen peroxide is a mild form of bleach. Do not use on nylon or on fabrics with a special finish. Dilute 1 part to 6 parts water.

Methylated spirit is a good last resort, if the gentler treatments haven't worked. Use neat and apply with a white cloth. Do not use on acetate or tri-acetate fabrics.

Salt removes blood stains and absorbs coloured liquid stains.

Washing soda is good for greasy stains.

White spirit attacks paint stains.

There are also proprietary kits of stain removers available which you might find useful.

Identifying fibres

Fabrics can only really be cleaned safely and successfully if you can identify the fibres in them. The simplest form of identification (unless there is a label to tell you) is to apply the burning test to a small piece of the fabric. Take a piece from the hem or a wide seam.

Cotton and linen will both burn with a yellow flame and leave a grey residue. Cotton smells a bit like burning paper and linen like burning grass.

Wool smells like burning hair and leaves tiny black bits.

Silk shrivels into a small scrap and smells unpleasant.

Most man-made fibres appear to melt and shrivel but the actual content is usually well labelled. For advice on how to look after fabrics made from man-made fibres see pages 186-187.

Fillings

Choosing fillings for cushion pads and pillows is very important, though you can buy ready-made cushion pads in department stores. However, the shape you want may not be a standard one.

Foam chips are probably the cheapest filling, but they are not ideal as they can look lumpy. Use a thick lining for your cushion pad so the lumps aren't so noticeable. They are non-absorbent.

Acrylic and polyester wadding is completely washable.

Kapok is a cotton fibre and can go lumpy after a time. It is non-absorbent.

Feathers make soft, beautiful cushions and retain their shape well. They are expensive, however.

Down is the most expensive filling and can be used with feathers to cut the cost.

Foam can be cut to shape and is ideal for larger cushions. Surround it with a layer of wadding to soften the outline. Cover foam shapes with a lining too as the foam will break down eventually.

STAIN REMOVAL

Alcohol   Mop up and dab with warm water and liquid detergent. Sponge again and blot.

Ballpoint pens   On washable fabrics, dab lightly at the stain with methylated spirit, then soak in a biological detergent and rinse. On non-washable items, treat with methylated spirit on cotton wool and dry clean professionally.

Blood   Soak washable items straight away in cold salt water and remove any stubborn stain with salt paste. Heat of any kind will seal the stain, so do not wash until every trace has gone. On non-washable items, spot with cold water mixed with a few drops of ammonia. Rinse with clear water.

Butter and other cooking fats   Scrape off surface deposit and use a proprietary stain remover. Dry clean.

Chocolate   On washable items, scrape off as much as you can, then dab the stain with soapy water with a few drops of ammonia in it. Wash in biological detergent. On non-washable fabrics, scrape off as much as possible and take to the dry cleaners.

Coffee   A natural dye so be swift. Washable items should be soaked in a biological detergent in hand-hot water. If the stain remains, try methylated spirit or mix a weak solution of 1 part 20 vol. hydrogen peroxide to 6 parts water. If the stain is old, equal parts of glycerine and warm water if left for a while may shift it. Rinse off. For non-washables, sponge up the coffee and try a stain remover.

Crayons and chalks   Washable items should be sponged with detergent mixed with water, having first brushed off any chalk or crayon deposit. Non-washable fabrics should be sent to the dry cleaners if possible.

Felt-tip pens   This ink has a different base to fountain-pen ink. Try dabbing methylated spirit on the fabric, but it is best to have it professionally dry cleaned.

Furniture polish   Fabrics should be treated with a stain remover.

Ink   Wash fabric thoroughly in cold water under a running tap. Apply neat liquid detergent, and if the stain persists, apply an equal mix of water, lemon juice and ammonia. Take non-washables to the dry cleaners or, if this is not possible, treat with a proprietary stain remover.

Lipstick   Scrape deposit off with a knife then rub vaseline or glycerine into the stain to loosen it. You could also try eucalyptus oil.

Mud   Allow the mud to dry, then wash in the usual way. Sponge non-washable items with a detergent solution and then use a stain remover.

Nail varnish   Remove from washable items with a non-oily varnish remover, working from the back of the fabric. Then use white spirit. Follow up with methylated spirit, if necessary. Take non-washable items to the dry cleaner's after cleaning up the spill with cotton wool or paper towels.

Paint   Treat as for nail varnish if it is gloss paint. Otherwise wash fabric in the usual way. Keep non-washables damp and dry clean immediately.

Tea   Soak washable fabrics in a solution of 1 tablespoon borax to 1 pint (560ml) water. Wash in the normal way. Old stains can be softened with equal parts glycerine and warm water. Treat non-washable items with the same borax solution and follow up with a proprietary stain remover.

GLOSSARY OF FABRIC NAMES

There is nothing so disheartening as going to all the trouble and expense of buying fabric to make curtains or loose covers, only to discover afterwards that it was not the best choice. Curtains that have sagged, or covers that shrank in the first wash, are dreaded possibilities only really avoided by researching before you buy. Here is a glossary of fabrics most frequently encountered in home furnishings, listed in categories of usefulness.

It is important to evaluate a fabric's weight and weave as well as its constituents. Polyester, for example, can be used to make a flimsy, sheer curtain or it might be manufactured in a heavier, closer weave, suitable for a tough deck-chair cover. The toughest weave, woven closely, is the plain weave, in which the weft and warp (cross and lengthwise) yarns are interwoven evenly. The hopsack or basket weave produces a looser fabric, two weft yarns weave over and under two warp yarns, making a softer fabric with more drape. Less durable weaves are twill and satin weaves, both having lengthwise yarns which skip over several crosswise yarns or vice versa.

Of course, the characteristics of the fibres included in the cloth also play a part. For instance, acrylic fibres are easy to wash, resistant to mildew, fading and creasing and cannot be attacked by moths. I have therefore included a list of the fibres and their qualities on pages 186-187.

The texture of a fabric also contributes to its usefulness. Candlewick is often used for bedcovers because it appears never to crease, but corduroy with the same corrugated texture, given time and wear, will be flattened if used on a cushion that is frequently sat upon, even though this is one of the toughest close weaves.

Finishes

There are chemical finishes which can be applied to fabric to improve its manageability. For example, linen has a tendency to crease, so it is often treated with a special chemical to improve its resilience. When you buy your furnishing fabric it is important to note whether it is a natural or a man-made fibre or a blend of both. The blend gives the best of both worlds allowing the beauty of natural fibres to be more easily cared for. However, man-made fibres do tend to create static electricity, which means they attract dirt.

All-purpose fabrics

The following fabrics can be used for curtains and covers of all kinds. Most of them are hard wearing and easy to clean. If you decide to use them on a dining seat or a headboard, they can be treated with a waterproof stain guard, usually marketed in an aerosol can.

Calico has a matt finish and is usually made of cotton. It is a mediumweight plain weave.

Cavalry twill (sometimes referred to as twill) is a medium- to heavyweight cloth with a herringbone weave which looks like a distinctive zigzag pattern. Traditionally it is made of wool, and now is sometimes woven in cotton or viscose, though any fibre can be woven in this way.

Chambray is a plain-weave, tough cotton fabric with a mottled appearance, looking rather like denim. The warp or lengthwise yarn is usually in a colour, and the weft or crosswise yarn is white or off-white. It is sometimes checked and striped.

Chintz is a good-quality, closely woven cotton fabric, often printed with large traditional bird and flower designs. It sometimes has a glossy glazed resin finish to resist dirt and is then called glazed chintz.

Canvas is a stiff, heavy fabric made of closely woven, unbleached, rough cotton. In lighter weights it is known as duck, and in medium weights, sailcloth. It is right for garden chairs and awnings, but except in the lighter weights it is not easy to sew.

Corduroy is a strong, cotton yarn fabric with distinctive pile ribs running its length. Needlecord is a lighter weight fabric of the same construction, not suited to covers, but it would make curtains. It creases.

Cretonne is often printed in patterns similar to chintz and is a hard-wearing cotton. It is not as finely woven as chintz and does not have the glossy finish.

Denim is a heavier twill weave variety of chambray and if made of all cotton or cotton with polyester, the fabric is firm, though it softens with wear. If made with more polyester and less cotton, it is softer and more crease resistant.

Gabardine is a very hard-wearing, mediumweight fabric with a distinctive diagonal rib formed by the twill weave. Traditionally made of cotton or wool, it is now made in all sorts of fibres including nylon, polyester, acrylic, viscose and cotton blends and, according to fibre content, it makes a tough fabric, even suitable for car seats.

Holland is plain-weave, mediumweight cloth made of cotton or linen which is very hard wearing. It is often stiffened and used for blinds.

Homespun has a loosely woven, hand-loomed look with a rather coarse yarn. It can be made in any weight and from any fibre. The heavier weights are suitable for upholstery.

Poplin is a hard-wearing, mediumweight, plain-weave cloth, traditionally made of cotton. It has a slight crosswise rib produced by interweaving a heavier crosswise yarn. When pronounced, it is referred to as rep. It has a slight sheen and creases, although less so if polyester yarn has been included.

Ticking is a tough, medium- to heavyweight twill weave especially made for bedding of all kinds. It is traditionally a cotton woven in a pattern of white and black or grey stripes, though it now comes in other colours too.

Tweed is a thick, slightly hairy fabric, best known in wool, made from rough-textured, randomly coloured yarns. It can be mixed with linen, cotton and other fibres.

Limited-use fabrics

These fabrics are not as hard wearing as the all-purpose group above. They are best for curtains, bedspreads and cushions, unless otherwise stated.

Bouclé is a knitted fabric with a knobbly look on the right side. It is usually medium weight and made of polyester, nylon and acrylic yarns.

Brocade is a medium- to heavyweight satin weave originally made in silk, sometimes with metal threads added. It looks like embroidered cotton cloth.

Chenille is any fabric made from a fringed or looped yarn. It does not crease and so is often used for bedspreads (candle-wick). Fibres may be cotton, viscose, silk or wool.

Damask is an ancient fabric first made of silk in Damascus. It is elaborately woven and often reversible. Now woven in many mixtures and weights. Linen damask, boiled, starched and given a gloss with an iron, makes smart tablecloths and napkins. However, all damask creases easily.

Faille is a fine, plain weave characterized by a crosswise rib produced by a thicker yarn. Traditionally made of silk, but now more likely to be acetate, viscose or polyester.

Moiré is a faille impressed with a water-marking effect which makes it look wavy. It is an effect which can be impressed onto other fabrics as well.

Muslin is a medium- to lightweight plain weave, traditionally in cotton. The finer quality muslins are used for table linen and the coarser, tougher variety for an undercover to upholstered furniture.

Percale is a close-weave cotton, similar to poplin, with a smooth, firm surface. It cleans and wears well and is excellent for sheets and quilt or duvet covers.

Sateen is similar in construction to satin but is generally made of cotton. It has a sleek, lustrous finish and in heavy weights can be used for loose covers and curtains.

Satin is not unlike sateen to look at but is far silkier to feel, and more usually in plain colours for furnishing. It is very slippery and requires careful pinning and basting.

Seersucker has puckered stripes alternating with flat stripes of different widths. Sometimes the stripes are multi coloured or a pattern can be printed. Traditionally made of cotton.

Shantung was traditionally made of slubbed silk yarn and now made from man-made fibres as well. It is like silk with a gentle, knobbly effect.

Taffeta was once made of silk but is now more likely to be made of acetate, tri-acetate, nylon or mixtures of these.

Terry towelling is a fabric with a looped pile, usually made of cotton. It is highly absorbent.

Velvet is a pile cloth made of silk and now from cotton, nylon, acetate and other man-made fibres. It can be produced with a crushed effect, or cut to produce raised patterns. When sewing, baste and machine stitch all seams in the direction of the pile. It is likely to pucker.

Velveteen is similar in looks to velvet, but is nearly always made of cotton. It has more body to it. Sew in the same way as you would velvet.

Sheer curtains

Most of these fabrics can be made into sheer curtains, but they can be backed with other fabrics to accentuate their pattern; lace or broderie anglaise, for example, backed with a darker fabric, makes a beautiful bedspread.

Broderie anglaise is a plain-weave cotton or polyester and cotton, in which shapes – leaves, flowers, circles – are punched and then satin stitched, giving the effect of open embroidery.

Lace is an open-work fabric in a variety of contructions and designs. Traditionally made of linen, but now most commonly in nylon, viscose or cotton.

Lawn is a lightweight, soft, fine cotton weave, now made in other fibres as well.

Leno is a type of weave in which the yarns cross to produce a figure of 8, giving an open-mesh effect that is very strong.

Marquisette is a loose, open fabric in a leno weave, which sometimes has dots or other designs included. It is made of cotton, silk or wool, but the most common fibres are now glass fibre nylon or polyester.

Net is an open-mesh fabric woven in diagonal twisted lines like a fishing net. Can be made of cotton and any kind of man-made mixture.

Organdie, traditionally made of cotton, is crisp and lightweight with a closely woven yarn.

Voile is a soft, plain weave made of fine, closely woven yarns. It is flimsy and fluid and drapes well.

Lining and stiffening fabrics

These fabrics are used to improve the appearance of curtains, bedspreads and pelmets, and to give extra body. Some are specially designed to add sunproofing and lightproofing qualities, and for extra warmth.

Buckram is a stiff, coarse-woven fabric made from cotton yarn and heavily sized to give it an almost rigid finish. Used for pelmets and tie-backs.

Domette is a soft open-weave fabric, mostly cotton, or a blend with cotton. It is used to interline curtains.

Non-woven stiffeners are made of matted synthetics. The come in different weights and look like white felt. Some have iron-on qualities.

Reflective lining is a mediumweight fabric coated on one side with a metallic finish that reflects heat and sun.

Sateen lining is a poorer quality than the sateen listed above. It is used for lining curtains.

Wadding is thick, soft cotton wadding sandwiched between two papery layers of shiny covering. It comes in various thicknesses or weights.

FIBRE CLASSIFICATION

FIBRE	ADVANTAGES
Acetate A man-made fibre made from cellulose.	Inexpensive and drapes well. Resistant to moths and mildew. Not exactly crease resistant but tends to spring back into shape. Good colour range.
Acrylic Soft, woolly, synthetic fibre. A generic term – other brand names include Acrilan, Orlon, Courtelle.	Resistant to abrasion, moths, mildew, sunlight and creasing. Keeps colours well and mixes well with other fibres. Will not stretch.
Cotton Extremely versatile and absorbent. Natural plant fibre.	Tough and abrasion resistant. Dyes beautifully producing an enormously varied range. Feels cool and is easy to wash. Has no static electricity. Mixes well with other fibres.
Glass A silicate fibre made specially to resist damage by the sun.	Resistant to moths, mildew and damage from sun. Colourfast and will not crease or shrink. Flameproof and stays free from static electricity.
Linen A very strong yarn with a high lustre made from flax fibres.	Can be used for all kinds of different weights and weaves to make fine lawn or heavy upholstery fabrics. Easy to clean. Feels cool and dyes well offering a superb colour range.
Modacrylic A man-made fibre even stronger than acrylic, often blended with other fibres and mixed with wool and cotton to improve performance and reduce cost.	Resilient and hard wearing with little elasticity or loss of shape. Crease resistant but holds pleats well. Not damaged by sun, moths, mildew, alkalis and acids. It is soft, warm and colourfast and comes in a good colour range.
Nylon Hard-wearing, man-made non-absorbent polyamide fibre produced from mineral sources (Perlon, Celon, Enkalon and Antron).	Extremely strong and resistant to moths and mildew. It has an inherent elasticity so it recovers its shape if stretched. It dyes well and comes in a good colour range. It blends well with other fibres. It is easy to clean and dries quickly.
Olefin A non-absorbent synthetic fibre, a by-product of petroleum.	Very strong and resistant to moths, mildew and stains. Crease resistant. Often recommended for outdoor use.
Polyester Extremely strong man-made fibre from petroleum chemicals. First sold by ICI as Terylene. Dacron, Chemstrand, Trevira and Crimpilene are later brand names.	Strong, resistant to abrasions, creases, moths and mildew. Dyes quite well and resists sunlight. Keeps its shape well. Often added to other fibres to make them easy to care for. Mixed with cotton sometimes.
Polyvinyl Chloride Often called PVC or vinyl coating fabric, it is a synthetic made from basic chemicals found in salt water and petroleum.	Can often be wiped clean, is very tough. Resistant to fading, mildew, fire and is weatherproof, though not waterproof.
Rayon (Viscose rayon) The oldest of the man-made fibres and the most versatile. Can be used for anything from underwear to carpets.	Strong and is not affected by the chemicals in household bleaches. Hangs well and has a good colour range.
Silk A natural fibre unwound from the cocoon of a silk worm. Luxurious, soft and warm.	Elastic and resilient, making relatively thin but hard-wearing fabrics possible. Feels cool, resistant to mildew and creases. Dyes particularly well. Exceptional range of colours.
Wool Natural fibres from the sheep's fleece. Usually absorbent, soft and hard wearing.	Warm and easy to manipulate. Strong and not damaged by the sun. Resists creasing and in close weaves resists abrasion. Dyes well and comes in a good colour range.

DISADVANTAGES

Melts at a low heat, not particularly hard wearing. Unless stated, it fades and is usually not washable. Not good in sunlight which weakens the fibre.

Accumulates static electricity and tends to pull.

Unless lined, it does weaken and fade in strong sunlight and may crease or shrink if not treated. It can also be attacked by mildew.

Requires special handling and care, as it can scratch and splinter. Colour range is limited and it has a poor resistance to abrasion. Can crack along the seams.

Unless treated, it shrinks and creases very easily. Colours tend to fade, especially in strong sunlight. It can stretch and shrink in damp conditions. Strong colours may run.

Tends to melt at a relatively low heat and has a poor resistance to abrasion. Prone to accumulate static electricity.

Tends to weaken and fade in sunlight and collects static electricity.

Collects static electricity. Inclined to fade and weaken in sunlight. Limited colour range.

Collects static electricity and sometimes puckers.

Limited colour range and melts at a low heat.

Non-washable, creases easily and lacks durability. It is affected by mildew, sunlight and abrasion.

Expensive and quite delicate in construction and weight. Fades and is weakened by sunlight. Can be damaged by abrasion and spotted by water.

Cannot usually be washed, will shrink unless labelled otherwise. Will be attacked by moths, so must be treated. Tends to collect static electricity.

TREATMENT

Iron on a low setting while slightly damp. Dry clean unless otherwise labelled. Do not apply methylated spirit to remove stains.

If washable, treat gently and use the appropriate setting on the washing machine – not above 40°C/104°F. The heat will set creases that will never come out. A fabric softener will help to control the build-up of static electricity.

Dry clean unless otherwise labelled colour fast and pre-shrunk, in which case it can be washed and pressed with a medium to hot iron.

Do not dry clean. Wash carefully by hand, wear rubber gloves. Drip dry. Do not tumble dry. Do not press.

Dry clean unless labelled pre-shrunk and colour fast. Iron while slightly damp. Avoid too much starching, which tends to damage the fibre.

Dry clean unless labelled colour fast, in which case wash gently. Drip dry and iron on a cool setting.

If labelled washable, wash separately, as nylon takes up other colours, otherwise dry clean. A fabric softener will help to control the static electricity. To avoid creasing remove immediately from a tumble dryer. Iron on a warm setting.

Dry clean unless labelled washable. Wash gently and tumble dry on a low heat setting. Use a fabric softener to control static electricity.

Dry clean, unless labelled washable. Wash gently and separate whites from other colours. Polyester tends to soak up loose colour pigments. Use a fabric softener to help control static electricity. Warm iron.

Hand wash carefully and avoid twisting, wringing or folding. Drip dry, do not iron. Do not dry clean, unless otherwise stated.

Dry clean unless labelled differently and press with a cool iron.

Dry clean unless otherwise stated and press with a warm iron from the wrong side.

Furnishing fabric should be dry cleaned. Steam press or iron with a warm iron.

INDEX

PICTURE CREDITS